Twayne's United States Authors Series

Sylvia E. Bowman, *Editor*

INDIANA UNIVERSITY

Sherwood Anderson

SHERWOOD ANDERSON

by **REX BURBANK**
San Jose State College

 65

Twayne Publishers, Inc.   ::   New York

51569

FOR
J. H., C. A. AND S. A.

Preface

SHERWOOD ANDERSON was admirably equipped, in range and variety of experience, to explore the possibilities and limitations of Midwestern American life. Restless by nature, he was almost an epitome of that peculiar American paradox by which swarms of nomadic people have searched for "roots," for a home. He knew firsthand the vague longings and dissatisfactions of the culturally deprived and inarticulate. He felt drawn, by turns, to the lusty excitement and dramatic turbulence of Chicago and to the elemental simplicity and dark mysteriousness of the Midwestern cornfields; to the sophisticated intellectuals of the Northern cities and to the Southern hill folk and Negro river hands. Conversely, he was repelled by the squalor and standardization of the new industrial metropolises; and he invariably became bored with the isolation and dullness of small-town and country life. And he was never comfortable for long in the company of fellow-artists, critics, or scholars; but among the simpler folk he felt the absence of intellectual stimulation.

In the dilemmas created by such incompatible demands upon his nature and in the wide-ranging facts of his life lay materials for penetrating literary analyses of American life; and Anderson was blessed with the natural endowment of talent necessary to transform those dilemmas into works of art. The first chapter of *Sherwood Anderson*, therefore, includes those facts of Anderson's life that shaped the essential configurations of his tales and romances and that formed the attitudes that became his themes. Thanks to two major biographical accounts of Anderson by Irving Howe and by James Schevill and to a number of doctoral dissertations, the facts of his life are generally well known. I have made extensive use of these sources, as well as much of the remainder of the large body of scholarship and criticism that has accrued particularly since Anderson's death.

In chapter 2, Anderson's two published apprenticeship novels, *Windy McPherson's Son* and *Marching Men* are shown to be early expressions of the symbolic rise to consciousness and quest for innocence of the Midwesterner that Anderson drew after his own life and used as the structural and thematic basis for his later work. The initial shadowings of the Naturalistic myth of the grotesque that was interwoven with the narrative showing the rise to moral consciousness—to conscience—of a hero are also traced in the second chapter, which provides a critical framework for the subsequent chapters in which specific works are analyzed.

Chapter 3 is a study of *Winesburg, Ohio* as a work in which Anderson emphasized the grotesque and used his narrative of emerging psychic and moral consciousness as an implied norm (as distinguished from a directly stated theme) with great effect and created an enduring masterpiece. This chapter also stresses the esthetic significance of Anderson's use of impressionistic techniques and the effects of those techniques in rendering his vision of human life.

Chapters 4 and 5 contain analyses of *Poor White* and of the tales in *The Triumph of the Egg* and in *Horses and Men*. These chapters are concerned largely with the varying degrees of Anderson's mastery of narrative perspective. They show how he combined techniques borrowed from Twain with the special elements of his own myth-theme in drawing the remarkable inner portrayals of groping innocents that have comprised his peculiar and unsurpassed contribution to the world of letters.

In chapters 6 and 7, *Many Marriages*, *Dark Laughter*, *Beyond Desire*, and *Kit Brandon* are examined from the standpoint of Anderson's growing concern with psychological and moral solutions to the problems of modern urban industrial society, a concern that presented formidable intellectual and esthetic difficulties from which the more objective and less prescriptive tales were relatively free. Chapter 7 also deals with *A Story Teller's Story* as a "confession" rather than as an autobiography, and it shows how Anderson, by using the confessional perspective of some of the better tales and the symbolic techniques of Henry Adams, achieved a measure of success he seldom enjoyed in his efforts in the romance-novel.

The concluding chapter discusses briefly Anderson's *Memoirs* as another "confession" and as a final expression of the American "myth" in which Anderson nearly recaptured the idiomatic style, prose rhythms, and poignant, nostalgic temper of *Winesburg, Ohio*. The final chapter also includes a summarized assessment of Anderson's work and its influence upon other American writers.

Scholars and critics and the reading public agree, generally, upon Anderson's failures as well as his successes; and it is not my intention in this book to bring up for revaluation such palpably bad efforts as *Many Marriages* or *Beyond Desire,* which neither historical change nor shifts in literary taste can resurrect. *Sherwood Anderson* is also not intended to upset commonly accepted evaluations of Anderson's finest achievements. My principal purpose has been twofold. First, I have sought to identify and define the sources and nature of Anderson's moral and literary heritage. While his influence upon subsequent American writers has long been acknowledged, the cultural factors that formed his attitudes and were ultimately felt in both his life and his works have not previously been drawn together and presented in the unified fashion in which, despite many cross-currents and contradictions, they present themselves. The course of Anderson's life and the structure of his longer narratives followed a discernible pattern which places him in a well-defined, indigenous literary and intellectual tradition, and for the most part his tales and romances may be assessed in terms of how much of that pattern he used and how consciously he used it.

Second, I have analyzed those works of Anderson's that represent his most important achievements and failures and that demonstrate the essential features of his art and development as a writer. Many of Anderson's works—such as *Tar: A Midwest Childhood* and a number of the tales in *Death in the*

Woods—do not require or do not deserve analysis; and I have made little or no mention of them in the belief that oblivion is the proper fate for some and that those still worth reading will generally be readily understandable to those readers who have grasped the meaning of the more significant works. Needless to say, no selection has been ignored because it failed to fit a preconceived thesis.

REX BURBANK

San Jose State College

Acknowledgments

I wish to express my appreciation to the American Philosophical Society for a grant to help me in my research on Anderson and to the San Jose State Foundation for assistance in procuring needed source materials and supplies. I am grateful once again to Professor Joe Lee Davis of the University of Michigan for valuable suggestions about approaches to Anderson. And to my wife Nancy I owe thanks for invaluable help and constant encouragement.

I also want to express my gratitude to the following persons and institutions for permission to quote from copyrighted materials:

To Mrs. Eleanor Anderson, for permission to quote from those of Anderson's works for which she holds copyrights.

To Harold Ober Associates, Inc., for permission to quote from *Poor White, A Story Teller's Story, Dark Laughter, Death in the Woods,* and *Sherwood Anderson's Memoirs.*

To The Viking Press, Inc., for permission to quote from *Winesburg, Ohio* and *Mid-American Chants* by Sherwood Anderson, and from Jean Stein's "Interview with William Faulkner" in *Writers at Work,* Series I, edited by Malcolm Cowley.

To Random House, for permission to quote from *The Autobiography of Alice B. Toklas* by Gertrude Stein, and from *The Age of Reform* by Richard Hofstadter.

To the University of Chicago Press, for permission to quote from *The American Adam* by R. W. B. Lewis.

To Little, Brown and Company, for permission to quote from *The Letters of Sherwood Anderson* edited by Howard Mumford Jones in association with Walter B. Rideout, copyright 1953 by Eleanor Anderson.

To Princeton University Press, for permission to quote from *The Intent of the Artist* edited by Augusto Centeno; and from *Anatomy of Criticism* by Northrop Frye.

To Oxford University Press, for permission to quote from *A Search for Man's Sanity: The Selected Letters of Trigant Burrow, with Biographical Notes,* copyright, 1958.

Contents

Chronology

1876   September 13, Sherwood Anderson born in Camden, Ohio; the third child of Irwin and Emma Anderson.

1884   Anderson family settled in Clyde, the factual original of Winesburg, Ohio.

1895   Emma Anderson died.

1896   Anderson left Clyde for Chicago, where he worked as a laborer in a warehouse.

1898   April, entered army for service during Spanish-American War, serving for a year.

1899   September, Anderson enrolled in Wittenberg Academy; graduated the following June.

1900   Returned to Chicago as advertising salesman and writer. For next five years, wrote advertisements and columns championing advertisements. First literary efforts.

1904   May 16, married Cornelia Lane of Toledo, Ohio.

1906   Moved to Cleveland as president of United Factories Company, a mail-order jobbing agency.

1907   Went into business in Elyria, Ohio. During the next five years wrote four novels: *Mary Cochran, Talbot Whittingham, Windy McPherson's Son,* and *Marching Men.*

1912   November, broke down under pressures of private and business life. Following recovery, left Elyria for Chicago.

1913-   Joined Floyd Dell, Margaret Anderson, Eunice Tietjens,
1915   Ben Hecht, Carl Sandburg, and others as part of "Chicago Renaissance." Wrote pieces for the *Little Review.*

1915-   Lived on Cass Avenue in Chicago and wrote the tales
1916   that were brought together as *Winesburg, Ohio. Windy McPherson's Son* (1916) published by John Lane after two years of effort by Floyd Dell and Theodore Dreiser

to find a publisher. Married Tennessee Mitchell (1916), and spent vacation with Waldo Frank and Trigant Burrow at Chateaugay Lake, New York. Anderson writing *Mid-American Chants*.

1917 *Marching Men* published by John Lane. *Winesburg* sketches being published by *Seven Arts*.

1918 *Mid-American Chants* published. Correspondence with Van Wyck Brooks and Waldo Frank comprised much of his literary education at this time; revealed Anderson's interest in Twain, Lincoln, and Whitman. Read with great interest *The Education of Henry Adams*.

1919 *Winesburg, Ohio*.

1920 *Poor White*.

1921 *The Triumph of the Egg*, a book of tales or "impressions" of American life, with cuts of busts by Tennessee Anderson and poems by Anderson. Met Ernest Hemingway. Made first trip abroad, met Gertrude Stein, James Joyce, Ford Madox Ford and others. Given the first *Dial* award of two thousand dollars.

1922- Spent first winter in New Orleans; *Many Marriages* and
1923   *Horses and Men*.

1924 *A Story Teller's Story*. Late 1923 and early 1924 spent in residence in Reno, where divorce from Tennessee became final in April, 1924. Married Elizabeth Prall immediately afterward.

1925 "The Modern Writer" and *Dark Laughter*, the latter prompting Ernest Hemingway to write his parody of Anderson, Gertrude Stein, Mencken and others in *Torrents of Spring*. Met William Faulkner in New Orleans.

1926 *Tar: A Midwest Childhood* and *Sherwood Anderson's Notebook*. Went on lecture tour.

1927 *A New Testament*, a book of prose-poems most of which had been written eight years earlier. Second visit to Paris, meeting Joyce and Gertrude Stein once more. Went on lecture circuit to help pay for farm and house near

Marion, Virginia. Bought and operated two local newspapers.

1929   *Hello Towns,* sketches from his two newspapers: the *Smyth County News* and the *Marion Democrat.* "Nearer the Grass Roots" and *Alice and the Lost Novel.* Divorced third wife.

1930-   Met Eleanor Copenhaver. Supported strikers at Danville,
1931   Virginia; commitment to proletarian causes began. *Perhaps Women* (1931).

1932   *Beyond Desire.* Joined Edmund Wilson, Lincoln Steffens, Dreiser, Dos Passos, Cowley, Matthew Josephson and others in calling for a "new order" and for a "temporary dictatorship" of the proletariat.

1933   *Death in the Woods and Other Stories;* married Eleanor Copenhaver.

1934   *Winesburg, Ohio* staged by Jasper Deeter's Hedgerow Theatre.

1935   *Puzzled America,* a collection of essays written during tour of depression-era America.

1936   *Kit Brandon,* his last romance-novel.

1937   Dramatic versions of *Winesburg, Ohio, The Triumph of the Egg* and *Mother* published. Elected to National Institute of Arts and Letters.

1941   Died at Colon, Panama Canal Zone, of peritonitis, while en route to good-will tour of South America.

1942   *Sherwood Anderson's Memoirs.*

CHAPTER *1*

The Modern Adam

THE ELYRIA, OHIO, *Evening Telegram* on December 2, 1912, reported that Sherwood Anderson, one of the town's most prominent citizens and head of the Anderson Manufacturing Company, had been found in Cleveland "dazed and unable to give his name or address." Anderson's condition, the paper said, was diagnosed by physicians as nerve exhaustion, which was caused by the "cares of the Anderson Manufacturing Company" and by the additional burden of literary work he had been carrying on for some time. As a businessman and an aspiring writer, Anderson had been trying for nearly six years to live simultaneously in the increasingly grim world of profits and losses and in the compulsive world of the imagination.

The strain of those incompatible efforts finally became too great, and one afternoon late in November, 1912, while dictating a letter to his secretary, he suddenly broke off in mid-sentence, walked out of his office, and trudged along the railroad tracks toward Cleveland where he was found a few days later wandering aimlessly and talking incoherently. After a short stay in a Cleveland hospital, he returned to Elyria; but his life as a small-town businessman was over. Three weeks later he left for Chicago, never to return to the Anderson Manufacturing Company. Separation from his family came not long after his departure from business. Shortly after his arrival in Chicago, he sent for his wife and three children, but within a year and a half he broke that last bond with what had become for him the stifling conventions of middle-class life.

With better than half his life behind him, Anderson embarked upon his career as a writer. His collapse under the pressures

of the middle-class life he had so assiduously pursued and attained was delayed in coming, but it had been in the making
since his youth, and the conflict that culminated in his breakdown and subsequent recovery comprehended some of the
fundamental American experiences and provided him with the
materials for some of the most penetrating analyses of mid-
American life in our literature. Most apparent, perhaps, his rise
from youthful poverty to a modest prosperity as a businessman
was a realization of the Horatio Alger myth, a fulfillment of
the cherished popular belief that hard work and personal virtue
would be rewarded with material success. But his subsequent
breakdown also gave him a basis in personal experience for the
expression of another characteristically American concept, for
it was easily transformed into conscious repudiation of success—
a traditional symbolic gesture of American literary idealism
which D. H. Lawrence called the "myth of America."

Already, in three of the four novels Anderson had written,[1]
he had portrayed the rejection of conventional society as a
deliberate moral act by his heroes—the hero of the unpublished
Talbot Whittingham, Sam McPherson of *Windy McPherson's
Son* (1916), and Beaut McGregor of *Marching Men* (1917)—
and all his subsequent novels were to be grounded in a narrative metaphor of social renunciation and moral rebirth. His own
desertion of business and family, necessitated by a genuine
psychic collapse, added the weight of natural compulsion to
the force of moral principle in McPherson and McGregor, and
henceforth in his romances separation from the materialism and
Puritan moralism of middle-class America was the initial step
to psychic as well as moral rebirth and finally to a new sense
of social communion.

Anderson's conflict also drew him into a number of representative social, historical, and geographical situations; for his
periodic movements back and forth from small country towns
to the burgeoning industrial metropolis of Chicago as a laborer,
a commercial writer, and a businessman gave him an abundance
of firsthand experiences with a broad cross-section of life in
the Midwest during its transition from the agrarian to the industrial era. As he moved through the spectrum of Midwestern

life, he accumulated the experiences and materials for the highly original and incisive portrayals of grotesque individuals found in *Winesburg, Ohio; The Triumph of the Egg; Horses and Men;* and *Poor White.*

The line between Anderson's life and works was a thin one, but any effort to sort out the facts of his life that most illuminate his fiction is perilous; for as his misnamed "autobiographies" show, he was often hostile to facts and commonly—at times, indeed, almost perversely—distorted or altered facts to suit his imaginative purposes. It is well known, too, that he consciously cultivated a legend about himself and his desertion of business which romanticized his life and influenced critical interpretations of his works. Yet a brief survey of his life will be useful to our study of his tales and romances because it reveals how the conflicting patterns of his life, both before and after 1912, did in fact shape the essential narrative features of his fiction and provide them with a moral framework. Our survey will be most profitable if seen in terms of the various roles Anderson adopted as he sought to create an identity for himself, roles which often conflicted with one another and generated the tensions that lie within his works.

I *A Midwest Boyhood*

In the opening chapter of the partly autobiographical *Windy McPherson's Son,* young Sam McPherson executes an unscrupulous but shrewd maneuver which enables him to outwit one of his youthful rivals in their competition for newspaper customers in the village of Caxton, Iowa. That achievement prompts the town intellectual, John Telfer, to exclaim, "Who says the spirit of the old buccaneers is dead? That boy didn't understand what I said about art, but he is an artist just the same!" Anderson's sketch of Sam in this episode sums up accurately one of the most important motivating factors in his own early life: the intense drive to bring order to a badly disorganized life. Initially a response to family poverty, the need for order which finally made him a writer manifested itself at first in a competitive struggle for success—perhaps the only avenue of escape for a boy of his time and circumstances. As time passed, however, his need for order took on psychological and ethical meaning, finally bringing him to the art of writing as a necessity to his well-being. It also provided him with the attitudes that were implicit in his later portrayals of grotesque, fragmentary persons struggling for wholeness and innocence in a spiritually undernourished society.

There was an abundance of disorder in his early life. He was born on September 13, 1876, in Camden, Ohio, the third of six children in the family of Irwin and Emma Anderson. During his first eight years the Andersons lived in a number of Ohio villages while Irwin searched for work as a harness maker. In 1884, the family at last settled in the little town of Clyde, where Sherwood spent his formative years and gathered the impressions of small-town life that became the chief source of his best work. Located in a rich cabbage- and corn-growing region, Clyde was an uninspiring collection of faded clapboard country stores and frame houses. Its unpaved streets were alternately muddy and dusty; and the seat of its "culture"—the Opera House—was, along with its sixteen saloons, the scene of frequent brawls.[2] Like most other small towns, Clyde was committed to the idea of progress, and it competed with the nearby towns for such commercial assets as railroad sidings and industrial plants in the belief that it was destined to become a great city. But, like thousands of other Midwestern hamlets, it lost the race for progress to towns that were more favorably located or more adept in attracting industry.

Largely because it was unspoiled by industry, it remained for Anderson, as Hannibal, Missouri, did for Mark Twain, a nostalgic symbol of pre-industrial innocence; and in his *Memoirs* (1942) he remembered Clyde as a "fair and sweet town." Its very lack of "culture" made it in many respects a good place for a boy, to whom rustic crudity was likely to be seen in terms of the vigor and romance of horse racing, the feverish excitement of county fairs, and the fierce primitive loyalty to the local baseball team. The broad, rolling Ohio countryside offered streams for fishing and swimming, beech woods for loafing and dreaming, and sprawling cornfields for the bucolic pleasures and furtive adventures of the small-town lad, for whom the idyllic boy's world of Tom Sawyer and Huckleberry Finn was by no means to be found only in books.

Clyde, however, differed in one important respect from the Hannibal, Missouri, of half a century before, for whereas the ante-bellum town of Twain's youth was a growing, new agricultural community with some of the robust energy and diversity of a frontier settlement, post-Civil War Clyde, Ohio, was an agricultural village which, long since settled, lay stagnant between an exhausted agrarian era and a nascent industrial age. Moreover, while Hannibal drew people like Twain's father from Eastern towns and cities in search of a new chance in life, Clyde, with other Midwestern villages of the late nineteenth century, was losing many of its young people to the cities. The great frontier vitality that still existed when Twain was a boy had vanished, and the New England Calvinism brought west by Clyde's early settlers had lapsed into a moribund, secularized moralism whose proprieties remained as conventions after their religious significance was lost.

Like Twain, Anderson was painfully conscious in later years of the dark side of life in his home town, and it is that dark side we see in *Winesburg, Ohio.* But where Twain saw the absurdities of an immature culture and could satirize it, Anderson saw the grotesqueness of a culture grown old and tired before it had a chance to grow up; and he saw not absurd people but defeated ones. His attitude toward Clyde was, therefore, always to be ambivalent: "There were horse races in our main street on winter afternoons," he recalled nostalgically in his *Memoirs,* "the streets cleared for them, and on winter nights, dances in country barns. Maple trees shedding their winged seeds on spring days when a breeze sprang up, creeks near town where boys went to swim. The terrible passionate curiosity of the young male concerning the young female." But, after the early years of youth, life in Clyde became less than idyllic, and he grew increasingly aware of the "old men, young men already failures in life—inspired ones, who from the beginning accepted failure, embraced it."[3]

A sense of failure was part of his heritage, for by all conventional standards his father was the epitome of the ne'er-do-well. But Irwin Anderson was at least partly the victim of economic cycles and historical changes. Like other harness makers of the late nineteenth century, he found the demand for his skill diminishing as industry moved into the Middle West, and he spent much of his time looking for work. The panic years of 1883 and 1893 were particularly hard for him, and he took what jobs he could find as a painter and a paper hanger; but these trades offered scarcely more work than harness making. He was away from home for long periods, wandering through the towns and farmlands of Ohio searching for employment—often supporting himself, if we can believe Sherwood's account of that period in *A Story Teller's Story*, by entertaining the rural folk with romantic tales or parlor skits for which he earned his meals and lodging. During the worst times he had no money to send home, and Emma was compelled to take in washings, while Sherwood and his elder brother Karl found odd jobs to help support the family.

The family's poverty—perhaps somewhat exaggerated by Anderson later in life, but nevertheless authentic and, at times, grim enough—was a result of Irwin's easy-going irresponsibility as well as of the encroachments of mass-production manufacturing and depressions. By Sherwood's accounts in the autobiographical *A Story Teller's Story* (1924), *Tar: A Midwest Childhood* (1926), and *Memoirs* (1941), Irwin was a wildly fanciful man, erratic by nature and given to spinning fantastic yarns which not only captivated village and country audiences but also signified his habit of running away from the hard economic facts and obligations that he should have faced as a father and a husband. While young Sherwood felt a certain pride in his father's gift as a tale-teller, he could not then accept Irwin's imaginative qualities as satisfactory substitutes for success as a provider for the family. He deeply resented the poverty and humiliation he believed Irwin's improvidence inflicted upon the family, and he was particularly bitter about the hardship it brought to Emma. His youthful feelings toward his father may be seen in his devastating portrait of Windy McPherson as a braggart and a fool whose absurd boasting brings disgrace to his family in the presence of the whole town of Caxton, Iowa, and whose drunkenness and negligence indirectly cause the early death of his overworked wife.

Not until much later in life could Anderson fully appreciate the garrulous Irwin and the rich imagination he had inherited from him. In *A Story Teller's Story*, he recalled more generously that his father was "made for romance" and that for him "there was no such thing as fact. It had fallen out that he, never having had the glorious opportunity to fret his little hour upon a greater stage, was intent upon fretting his hour as best he could in a money-saving prosperous corn-shipping, cabbage-raising Ohio village."[4] While Anderson's attitude toward his father, like his feelings toward Clyde, grew more tender as time softened the remembrance of hardship and as maturity turned embarrassment to tolerance and understanding, Irwin remained for him a grotesque figure, a fragmentary personality whose defeated dreams of romance and heroism made him an oddity in the practical rural Ohio community. It is worth noting, in connection with Anderson's attitudes toward those defeated by life—as seen in such works as *Winesburg* and "The Egg"— that his later tolerance and sympathy for his father grew concurrently with a change from his earlier belief that Irwin himself was responsible for his "failure" in life to the conviction that his father was made grotesque by the society in which he lived. It is also significant that he himself was later compelled to abandon the responsibilities that as a boy he condemned his father for failing to accept.

Irwin's imprudence taught his son at an early age the facts of practical necessity, and Sherwood responded eagerly to the family's needs. He worked as a paper boy, a race-track swipe, and an errand boy; and his willingness to take on whatever work presented itself, his enterprise at creating jobs for himself, and his determination to apply himself diligently to whatever task he undertook gained him the nickname "Jobby" from the approving townsfolk. With reasonable allowance for exaggeration, we may assume that the energetic, serious, imaginative young Sam McPherson is an essentially correct portrait of Anderson the ambitious go-getter as a youth. Like Sam, Anderson was impressed while very young with the value of "getting ahead"; and, although at the age of forty-eight he could say that "Those who are to follow the arts should have a training in what is called poverty" rather than a "comfortable middle-class start in life," the economic and social facts of his boyhood impelled him, as they do Sam McPherson, toward pursuit of middle-class comfort rather than a career in the arts.

Though his attendance at school was irregular, he seems not to have regretted it until later when his lack of formal education became a handicap to him in finding a desirable job. Despite his sporadic schooling, however, he was not unacquainted with books, and there is no reason to doubt the validity of his later portrayals of himself, in *A Story Teller's Story* and *Tar*, as a boy who read widely, if unsystematically and without discrimination, and was—like Irwin—wildly imaginative. James Fenimore Cooper was one of his boyhood favorites, and with his playmates he enacted again and again the heroic adventures of the intrepid Hawkeye and the shrewd and daring Uncas. Like his elders in the drab Midwestern towns and on the isolated farms, he craved heroism and romance; and he eagerly absorbed the popular idealized biographies of Lincoln, Napoleon, and Jesse James, probably without bothering to make ethical distinctions among the heroes. His youthful thirst for romance and heroism took him to Walter Scott, Mark Twain, Jules Verne, and the ubiquitous dime novels, as well as to Cooper. Later, as he moved on into middle-class life, he developed a taste for books about people with "comfortable problems" and found his way to Howells, Stevenson, and Harriet Beecher Stowe. Ultimately— and we may safely surmise that it was after 1900—he "fed his dreams" with Shakespeare, Fielding, Balzac, Crane,[5] and Dreiser, whose *Sister Carrie* was republished in 1911 after ten years of suppression.

Youthful fancy and economic necessity were by no means mutually exclusive demands in the young Anderson, for he was intensely devoted to his mother, and the need for money in the Anderson household and his own proclivity for romance found a common ideal in the overburdened Emma Anderson. To Sherwood, Emma seemed to have all the desirable qualities that his father lacked; and, as he rejected Irwin's irresponsibility, he embraced the qualities of stoic endurance, self-sacrifice, and sympathetic curiosity that, to his mind, his mother possessed. Emma Anderson gave the family what little stability and security it had. Although Anderson's imaginative re-creations of her in *Tar* and *Dark Laughter* (1925) confer upon her a silent mysteriousness, a shrewd ingenuity, and a quiet courage, in excess, perhaps, of what she actually had, she seems to have had those qualities in abundance; and, if his later accounts of her were not factually true, they were to him essentially true. In *Windy, A Story Teller's Story* and *Tar* we see in the characters drawn after her the quiet, stoic courage and the inner calm and determination before adversity that he attributed to her.

Such virtues command the kind of devotion that can readily transform necessity into a moral ideal, and the fanciful Sherwood had no difficulty in embellishing his mother with romance and mystery. "Mother was tall and slender and had once been beautiful," he wrote in *A Story Teller's Story*. "She had been a bound girl when she married father. . . . There was Italian blood in her veins and her origin was something of a mystery. Perhaps we never cared to solve it—wanted it to remain a mystery."[6] While his account of her origin is surely apocryphal, Emma always represented to Sherwood an admirable outer inscrutability and an inner wisdom and certitude gained from a lifetime of hardship and suffering. He credited her with instilling in him her own penetrating insight and sympathetic understanding of people, and, in the dedication of *Winesburg, Ohio,* he acknowledged that her "keen observation on the life about her first awoke" in him "the desire to see beneath the surface of lives. . . ."

But despite her moral qualities, Emma Anderson remained to Sherwood a symbol of broken dreams, of a life spent in a dreary routine of washing and cooking and childbearing, a life starved for affection from her husband and devoid of adventure and excitement. No amount of romantic adornment could hide from him the grim fact of her neglect by Irwin and the burdens she bore almost alone. In view of his intense feelings about the uncomplaining Emma, it is readily understandable why Anderson was always to have the tenderest regard for the obscure "little" people defeated by life. In his most moving portrayals of her, in "Mother" and in "Death" in *Winesburg*, she is shown wasting away spiritually as well as physically in a life which was barren of intimate and significant adult human relationships. To Sherwood she embodied the most pathetic and beautiful qualities of the grotesque; a woman broken by a hard and sterile environment, by the callous disregard shown by others, and by the reticence and passiveness that accompanied such of her virtues as stoic and uncomplaining resignation, she was a prototype of the lonely person whose inner beauty "shines forth" in a strangely twisted fashion.

After Emma died of tuberculosis in 1885 at the age of forty-three, Anderson stayed in Clyde for about a year and then left for Chicago where he found a job as a stock handler in a warehouse. It was heavy work and particularly onerous to the slightly built Anderson. He soon found that Chicago offered a workingman scarcely more opportunities for improvement than the small farm-towns. While he was fascinated by the dramatic turbulence of the big city, he discovered—as Beaut McGregor does in *Marching Men*—that, for Chicago's swarms of wage-earners, life consisted of much the same dispiriting routine, dullness and hardship he had seen in Clyde. He instinctively loathed the depressing atmosphere of grimy houses, the soot-filled air, the dark and squalid streets and alleys of the great city. In *Marching Men*, in *A Story Teller's Story* and in such notable tales as "The Man's Story" (*Horses and Men*), he gives us a picture of Chicago as he saw it then: drearily standardized people, bitterly lonely and isolated from one another, who occasionally interrupt an otherwise unchanging routine of work with fighting and bickering or with inept attempts at love-making.

The Spanish-American War in 1898 gave Anderson a welcome opportunity to escape the grim, lonely life of a Chicago workman and to join in the excitement of the impending war in Cuba, so he returned to Clyde and enlisted in Company I of the Sixteenth Ohio National Guard Regiment, which shortly was taken into the United States Army. After seven and a half months of training in camps in Georgia and in Tennessee—where he saw for the first time the possibilities, depicted in *Marching Men*, of collective order in men marching together in a common cause—he was sent to Cuba in January, 1899, nearly six months after Spain had surrendered.

His ridiculously useless part in that war was at best a temporary escape from the hard routine of the workingman. He shared with his fellow infantrymen in Company I a hero's reception when he returned to Clyde in May, but after this brief moment of glory he was confronted once more with the cold necessity of making a living. He had no desire to return to his warehouse job in Chicago, and there was little reason to remain in Clyde, for his sister Stella and younger brothers Earl and Irving were in Chicago, and his elder brother Karl was living in Springfield. Only his brother Ray, to whom he was not close, and his father, with whom he had little to do, still lived in Clyde. With no family ties in Clyde and concerned that his lack of education would mean a lifetime as a day laborer, Anderson turned to Karl, an illustrator for the *Woman's Home Companion*, for advice about his future. When Karl advised him to enroll in the Wittenberg Academy in Springfield for the fall term, Anderson returned to Clyde, worked on a farm on the outskirts of town during the summer, and enrolled in the Academy in September.

In Springfield he lived in a boardinghouse called "The Oaks," where he earned his living expenses by running errands and doing odd jobs. Besides Karl, "The Oaks" included among its boarders a group of teachers, writers and artists who created what was for Anderson a lively and stimulating intellectual atmosphere. Biographer James Schevill observes that "Discussions about everything, from Nietzsche, education, and religion to the rise of the new advertising business, resounded through the house,"[7] and the likeable and impressionable Sherwood was welcomed into the discussions. He was fascinated by the clash of ideas, and, though there is no indication that they permanently influenced him, he seems to have been impressed for the first time with the possibility of a broader range of intellectual alternatives than he had been aware of. In school he found himself in classes with boys several years younger than himself, but he was an able if not brilliant student; and, in spite of the demands of his job at the boardinghouse, he achieved a scholastic record of eleven "A's" and three "B's" in a curriculum that included English, Latin, German, physics, and geometry.[8] He took an active part in the Athenian Literary Society, and at commencement in June, 1900, he spoke impressively on the subject of Zionism.

Anderson seldom mentioned his year at Wittenberg later in life, and, when he did, he referred to Wittenberg College rather than to the Academy, creating the impression that he had had a year of college when actually he never had any formal education beyond high school—a fact which suggests that the persistent and uncritical anti-intellectualism he later tried to cultivate as a virtue was at least partly a result of his sensitiveness about his own educational limitations. Nevertheless, the year at Wittenberg was a pleasant one for him, and he found the intellectual life—elementary though it probably was—enjoyable, though, as Irving Howe has observed,[9] there is little evidence in his manuscripts and letters to show that Anderson ever learned to spell, mastered a foreign language, or understood the authentic demands of science.

His incipient cultural development was arrested suddenly when his fellow boarder at "The Oaks," Harry Simmons, advertising manager for the Crowell Publishing Company, offered Anderson a job in Chicago. Impressed by Sherwood's commencement speech, Simmons asked him to take a position in the Chicago office of the *Woman's Home Companion.* For the ambitious Sherwood—now twenty-three—the prospect of returning to Chicago as an advertising man, where only two years before he had rolled barrels in a warehouse, must have seemed like a personal realization of the Horatio Alger legend, and it is little wonder that he soon found it easy to embrace the idealistic cant of the success ethic and to become a professional apologist for it.

After a short stay with the Crowell firm, he took a job with the Frank B. White Agency, which in 1903 merged with the Long-Critchfield Company. He wrote and sold copy for the next three years, and steeped himself in the commercial piety of advertising with an enthusiasm that must have warmed the hearts of even its most ardent apostles. His salary increased steadily, and he assiduously devised for himself the role of a business dandy. "I now advance rapidly," he recalled in his *Memoirs*. "I have twenty-five dollars a week, then thirty-five, forty, fifty, seventy-five. I buy new clothes, hats, shoes, socks, shirts. I walk freely on Michigan Boulevard in Chicago, go to drinking parties, meet bigger and bigger businessmen."[10]

Singing the praises of business and businessmen paid off in terms of reputation as well as money. Marco Morrow, another ex-boarder at "The Oaks" and the editor of a company trade publication called *Agricultural Advertising*, asked Anderson to contribute to the periodical, and during 1903 and 1904 he submitted several articles and copy for two monthly columns, each of which ran for ten months, called "Rot and Reason" and "Business Types." These pieces indicate the extent to which he was committed to the simplistic gospels of business and advertising. The following passage, for instance, rivals the most sanctimonious blandishments of George F. Babbitt and his "poet" friend Chum Frink: "One good, clean-minded businessman, who gets down to work cheerfully in the morning, who treats the people about him with kindness and consideration, who worries not about world-politics, who faces the small ills of his day. . . . is probably doing more downright good than all the canting moralists who ever breathed. . . ."

To the advertising man he attributed the courage, dedication, and patient endurance of the artist or missionary whose noblest efforts are confronted everywhere by ignorance, insensitivity and pagan disbelief: "A most hopeful, cheerful beggar he is, the advertising man, seeing his hardest licks go smash, his cleverest lines muddled and his finest talk interrupted. . . . Day after day, week after week, year after year, he faces his own failures and yet believes down in the heart of him that he is in the greatest business on earth and that next year will set all straight and turn all his penny marbles into diamonds."

Years later he remarked, perhaps with more pride than self-disparagement, that as a man of business he was a "smooth son of a bitch." Yet interwoven with the huckster's oily persuasiveness was an unmistakable desire to believe in the moral value of what he was doing. In his *Memoirs* he could point— with more than a little of the convert's smugness—to his early sins with proper contrition: "I create nothing. I boost, boost. Words of glowing praise for this or that product of some factory flow from under my pen."[11] But there was no skepticism at the time; and, beneath the obvious absurdity of such efforts to sanctify the businessman and his hired propagandist, there is a less apparent but more significant attempt to articulate an ideal. That need for an ideal, for a moral and ethical justification of his efforts, impinged with increasing force upon Anderson in the years before 1912 and contributed heavily—as it met continued frustration—to his collapse.

On May 16, 1904, he married Cornelia Lane of Toledo. Coming from a solid middle-class family, Cornelia represented to Anderson respectability, that indispensable adjunct to success which the middle class automatically grants to the family man. More important, she secured his new social station in life, for she enjoyed all the refinements of a middle-class upbringing which he had lacked and which were a part of the bourgeois ideal he desperately wanted to achieve. "You see," he wrote in his *Memoirs,* "the woman that I married was educated. She had traveled in Europe while I . . . . to tell the truth I could at that time just spell the simplest words—I was a man just out of the laboring class and to the American middle class that was then, and is perhaps yet, a disgrace."[12]

In September, 1906, he moved to Cleveland as head of the United Factories Company, a mail-order firm whose advertising account he had handled for Long-Critchfield. A year later, when his first child, Robert Lane Anderson, was born, Anderson decided to go into business for himself in the town of Elyria, which he had visited a number of times on business trips. There he soon became known as the "Roof-Fix Man," selling roof cement and paint by mail order.

The first years in Elyria seemed to be happy ones for both Sherwood and Cornelia as they lived the settled life of the respectable young couple. Two more children were born, John Sherwood on December 31, 1908, and daughter Marion on October 29, 1911. The Andersons attended church regularly and belonged to the country club; they entertained in the most genteel fashion and discussed the colleges to which they would send their children. They were a popular couple, acceptably ambitious and properly social; and Sherwood was generally regarded as a "sound" businessman. All was not as it seemed, however, for Anderson's vaunting commercial idealism underwent startling changes in Elyria. In 1909-10, he devised a plan he called "Commercial Democracy," whereby he hoped to give every man an opportunity to go into business selling Anderson's roof-fix (supposedly earning fat profits for Anderson as well) under an agency system similar to that of the United Drug Company and its Rexall chain.[13] At about the same time he wrote a pamphlet titled "Why I am a Socialist," which he destroyed but which marked a radical change in his social and moral outlook.

Accompanying this change in attitude toward business was a growing obsession with writing, and he spent increasing amounts of time at night in an attic room working on the four novels he completed before returning to Chicago. As writing became more and more of a necessity, he began to neglect his family and business; and by mid-1912 his personal and business affairs were in a precarious condition. But, though a number of his business associates and neighbors considered him rather queer for spending so much of his time writing stories, no one appears to have suspected that he was on the verge of a breakdown. Moreover, the degree to which his business acumen was respected is indicated by the fact that in 1911 he was able to persuade a group of local merchants and professional men to put up $200,000 to capitalize a new paint and roofing enterprise. It was this firm—in which he had invested no money of his own—that he abandoned in 1912.

In retrospect, it is clear that Anderson's breakdown was a result of the inexorable demands of his inner nature for freedom from the pressures and routines of business and family life. But it is equally clear that his conflict was moral as well as psychological; for, while the relative disorder and conflicting values of his youth were initially responsible for his eager acceptance of the simple-minded commercial ideals of the advertising business, other factors, inherent to his nature and deeply imbedded in his agrarian heritage, began—it must have been in about 1906—to undermine those shaky ideals and ultimately to destroy them. Certainly, Anderson was the heir of his father's highly imaginative nature, which could not long subsist on a thin commercial diet; and just as certainly he inherited Emma Anderson's intense curiosity about people, a curiosity that required—in the son as in the mother—a close, sympathetic relationship with friends that a casual, axe-grinding business fellowship could not provide. But equally important, he retained many of the attitudes of the small-town atmosphere in which he grew up: the sympathy for the "little" people beaten by life, the deep admiration for the authentic skill of the craftsman and the tradesman, and the agrarian disposition that could not value highly the unproductive efforts of the "middle-man" class. The driving energy of the ambitious "Jobby" and the slick self-promoter of the Anderson Manufacturing Company needed the sanction of a moral world. He built that moral world for himself as a writer in Chicago.

II *Primitive Bard*

Though a broken, defeated man when he left Elyria early in 1913, the ten years in Chicago from 1913 to 1923, Anderson later declared, were the happiest of his life. He regarded the period as one of rebirth for him, and he often cited Conrad's statement that "A writer is no older than his first published book" as applicable to himself in this second phase of his life.

His recovery and happiness in Chicago are easily explained, for there he did his best work and enjoyed his most vital, though not in all cases his most enduring, friendships. When he arrived from Elyria, he was desperately in need of companions who shared his dedication to writing and who did not question his judgment in abandoning his obligations in Elyria. Late in 1913 he was near nervous collapse once more, largely because of a conflict between his desire to dissolve finally his tie with Cornelia and his reluctance to abandon responsibility for his family. When he broke that tie in mid-1914 and Cornelia left to take a schoolteaching job in Indiana, his relief in being free was overshadowed by a nagging sense of guilt. He was convinced that the break was necessary, that he and Cornelia lived in separate worlds, and that there was no longer any hope for their marriage. He explained in his *Memoirs* that ". . . my first wife, the mother of my children, had been unable to believe in me as an artist and I could not blame her. She was a woman who, having married one sort of man, had awakened to find that she had got another." But in spite of his credible-enough rationalization and magnanimity, his final separation from Cornelia and the children bothered him, and he continued for several years to avoid any public mention of it.

In Chicago he found the "feeling of brotherhood and sisterhood with men and women whose interests were [his] own." This feeling sustained him through his personal crisis, and for the first time in years he was able to develop friendships that were free of commercial self-interest.

His literary education was concurrent with his new friendships. Initiation into the group which comprised the "Chicago Renaissance" came shortly after Karl Anderson, who was then in Chicago, took the manuscript of *Windy McPherson's Son* to Floyd Dell in the spring of 1913. Favorably impressed, Dell wrote an article in praise of Anderson in the "Friday Review of Literature," the literary supplement of the *Evening Post.* Through Dell's ex-wife, Margery Currie, Sherwood soon met Dell personally and was subsequently introduced to Ben Hecht, Arthur Davison Ficke, and Eunice Tietjens. That summer, Hecht—then a reporter for the *Daily News*—introduced him to Carl Sandburg (whom they nicknamed "John Guts" because he "wrote poetry that not only did not rhyme but yapped violently and mystically at life");[14] to Burton Rascoe who was reviewing books for the *Tribune;* and to Lewis Galantiere, then writing in Chicago.

At gatherings in Dell's rooms Anderson heard discussions ranging from socialism to the new theories of Freud and the genteel literary realism of Howells. Dell, a militant socialist and ardent pacifist, was the intellectual leader of the group until he left for New York late in 1913 to join Max Eastman on the radical *Masses*. He was steeped in Freudian psychology as well as socialism, and one of the favorite parlor games at his place was "psyching." "Freud had been discovered," Anderson recalled, "and all the young intellectuals were busy analyzing each other and everyone they met. Floyd Dell was hot at it."[15] At these sessions Anderson listened attentively; when he spoke, it was usually to tell a story.[16] Typically, his thinking was expressed in narrative rather than in conceptual terms, and, while he was in sympathy with socialist and Freudian concern about social and psychological repressions, he did not then and never did accept the idea that life could be shaped or explained by theories, an attitude he set forth most persuasively in "Seeds."

After the departure of Cornelia, Anderson took an attic room in a boardinghouse on the corner of Cass and Michigan Boulevard, where he met a number of aspiring actors, painters and dancers whom he later called the "little children of the arts." The area was a Chicago counterpart of New York's Greenwich Village, a neighborhood of multi-storied Victorian houses occupied in the 1890's by the well-to-do but now fallen into decay and converted into boardinghouses. Most of Anderson's fellow-boarders were hopeful amateurs, with a good deal more aspiration than talent; but his contacts with them were profitable, for a number of them became prototypes for characters in his tales. His stay in his gloomy attic room in that house was a happy one for the world of letters, for there he wrote *Winesburg, Ohio*.

In the years after 1914, he formed friendships with Harry Hansen, Ferdinand Schevill, Robert Morss Lovett, and Roger Sergel. With Hecht he drank beer at Schlogl's restaurant and listened to discourses on Dostoevski, Flaubert, and the French Symbolists. At an old store near Jackson Park that formerly belonged to Thorstein Veblen but at this time served as a gathering place, he heard Margaret Anderson, the strong-willed editor of the *Little Review*, talk at length about Gertrude Stein and James Joyce; and he also learned about the vital new work of Anatole France, Shaw, Strindberg, Schnitzler, and the post-Impressionist painters. He became a bohemian—just as, ten years before, he had become a "dandy." Devising a role for himself, he then shaped his habits to fit the role. He let his hair grow, wore strips of bright-colored cloth instead of neckties, and frequented Jack Jones' Dill Pickle Club, where he hobnobbed with bums, hoboes, political anarchists, and university professors.

Harry Hansen recalled "quiet talks with him in basement restaurants, sought out for the food or the red wine, but more often because Anderson had found the human side interesting. He would have talked with the owner, or his wife, about their homely cares, their inner hopes. He knew people either desired something very much and couldn't get it, or that desire was dead; and he was most sensitive to the promptings of appetite, hunger, and 'the perpetual tragedy of fulfillment.' . . . His sensuousness was not mere appetite, but a sort of basic means of communication and understanding with all human beings. He let people talk without interruption, not so much to hear the words they used as to speculate what lay behind them, for he felt that many of the words are not innately our own but inexact devices for our thoughts."[17]

The effect of his deep involvement with people in Chicago was decisive in both his life and his work, and sympathetic communion with others became a virtual creed for him.

In defining his role and his creed, he had the aid of Walt Whitman. Like Whitman, Anderson conceived of his poetic function as that of secular priest, or "divine literatus," the restorer of primitive sentience and the champion of the instincts and vibrant life of nature. In the "Mid-American Songs," which he began writing about 1916 and published as *Mid-American Chants* in 1919, he proclaimed his wholeness as a poet and declared that through his songs he would answer the "hunger within"—the loneliness and isolation that were the human lot in life. "I shall bring God home to the sweaty men in the corn rows," he wrote to Waldo Frank in May, 1917. "My songs shall creep into their hearts and teach them the sacredness of the long aisles of growing things that lead to the throne of the God of men."

It is likely that the songs reached scarcely more than the few hundred *Little Review, Poetry,* and *Seven Arts* subscribers and the handful of reviewers who, with good reason, read them with a general lack of enthusiasm. The sweaty men among the corn rows never heard of them. But more important to his art than his aim of curing the ills of a spiritually exhausted Midwest, was Anderson's emphasis upon the acceptance and absorption of all experience, which he implied in such lines as the following:

> Do you not see, O my beloved, that I am become strong
> to caress the woman! I caress all men and all women.
> I make myself naked. I am unafraid. I am a pure thing.
> I bind and heal.

The desire to "bind and heal," like the desire to reform society, was not only to remain with him for the rest of his career but was to pose serious problems in his fiction. But the Whitmanesque process of imaginative projection into the lives of others and sympathetic absorption of all life was to provide both the esthetic and the moral basis of his greatest work, *Winesburg, Ohio,* wherein the old writer in "The Book of the Grotesque" populates his imagination with the fragmentary lives of others and thereby makes himself psychologically and morally whole. The hero, young George Willard, weaves the fabric of his literary career out of his impressions and growing sympathy for the village grotesques.

Though his *Chants*—which show the influence of the Old Testament as well as of Whitman—did nothing to enhance his reputation, the bardic pose behind them and the sympathetic imaginative insight they expressed and exemplified were, like the act of writing, "curative" for Anderson; and psychologist Trigant Burrow, whom he met at Chateaugay Lake, New York, in 1916, later declared that Anderson was socially "one of the healthiest men" he had ever known.[18] Success accompanied his restoration to health, and the years 1917 to 1921 were the most productive of his career. He followed *Winesburg, Ohio* with two volumes of short stories, *The Triumph of the Egg* (1921) and *Horses and Men* (1923); two novels, *Poor White* (1920) and *Many Marriages* (1923); and a book of prose-poems similar to the *Mid-American Chants* titled *A New Testament* (1927).

His efforts during this period were climaxed by financial and critical success which, though modest by popular standards, marked his arrival as a serious writer. In 1921 the *Dial* presented him an award, its first, for his "service to letters," an honor which included a prize of two-thousand dollars that ultimately helped free him from his job with the Critchfield agency. His reputation—among critics, if not with the public—reached its apex in 1922 when Paul Rosenfeld wrote perceptively and approvingly of his development as an artist in the *Dial,* Lawrence Gilman called *The Triumph of the Egg* an "American masterwork" in the *North American Review,* and Mencken—who had earlier expressed doubts about what he regarded as Anderson's excessive absorption with sex and inability to master form—wrote enthusiastically about him in the *Smart Set.* His fame had already crossed the Atlantic. Early in 1923, Soviet translator Peter Ochremenko informed him that *The Triumph of the Egg* had been translated into Russian and asked permission to translate other works; and translations of *Poor White* and *Winesburg* into German and Czechoslovakian were to follow shortly.

In spite of his growing success, Anderson was by no means without problems and frustrations during this time. For one thing, he was still plagued by the necessity of working at the advertising office, and he complained bitterly that the best hours of his days were wasted in writing "stupid advertisements." In 1919 he felt so pressed for time and money that he asked Burrow for help in finding a patron who could give him "from twenty-five hundred to three thousand a year" to support himself and his children.[19] He also declared to Waldo Frank that he was determined to quit his job and prepared to "suffer what loss of friendship and what ugly hatred [were] necessary."[20]

But he was sustained in his work by the generous interest of his second wife and of three young Eastern scholars. In 1916 he married Tennessee Mitchell, a former schoolteacher from Michigan, whom he met in Chicago. While their "modern" marriage (they resolutely lived their own lives, maintaining separate living quarters) deteriorated badly after 1921—when Anderson began to enjoy better days—and ended in divorce in 1923 and heartbreak for her, Tennessee gave him both the emotional assurance and the liberty he needed during that discouraging but prolific period in his life. An aspiring sculptor herself, she shared with Anderson a deep commitment to art; and, despite her determined and visible displays of feminine independence, her own engrossed involvement with Anderson's work is indicated by the fact that she sculptured the busts of the chief characters of *The Triumph of the Egg.*

He was also fortunate at that time in commanding the interest of Van Wyck Brooks, Waldo Frank, and Paul Rosenfeld—three astute Eastern critics who gave him critical guidance and encouragement at a time when he had exhausted the thin cultural and literary resources of Chicago and was in need of both the assurance and authoritative judgment of the more exacting Easterners. Frank and Rosenfeld gave him all the personal warmth and approbation he required to sustain him through his moods of self-doubt; and the cold and aloof Brooks helped him understand and articulate the causes of his problems as an American artist.

With the advent of success and growing self-assurance, however, sophistication began to infringe upon Anderson's bardic role. In his correspondence with Frank, Rosenfeld, and Brooks prior to 1920, Anderson took noticeable pains to emphasize his adopted role as child of nature, counseling his friends against excessive intellectualism and cultivating the impression of himself as "a peculiarly windblown man" whose firsthand experience and whose intuition gave him access to areas of life untouched by the scholarly Easterners. By 1921, there was a perceptible change in his part from bardic singer to sophisticated cultural critic who could theorize to Rosenfeld, "I have a feeling that the great basin of the Mississippi River, where I have always lived and moved about, is one day to be the seat of the culture of the universe."[21] Partly a response to the growing sophistication of post-World War I American writing—as exemplified best, perhaps, by James Branch Cabell's suppressed *Jurgen*—Anderson's change was largely a result of his growing success and his desire to move away from the themes of "adolescence" in *Winesburg,* in *The Triumph of the Egg,* and in *Horses and Men* and into those which dealt with "problems."

III   *The Urban Sophisticate*

Despite his insistence that *Many Marriages,* which he began writing in 1920, was a "rollicking, Rabelaisian" novel that "ain't going nowhere," that book, dealing with a businessman who abandons his family and business and runs off with his secretary, was clearly an attempt to write in a sophisticated fashion on adult materials about social problems. As such it represented a reversion by Anderson to the type of "thesis" work he had done in *Windy* and in *Marching Men.* Reflecting the preoccupation with sex of the Freud-entranced 1920's (though Anderson was not himself influenced directly by Freud), *Many Marriages* was a deliberate affront to Puritan sex morality and a "case" for "blood consciousness," a radical change in perspective from the groping innocents of *Winesburg,* of *The Egg* and of *Horses and Men.* Like *Many Marriages, Dark Laughter* (1925) reflected Anderson's change in role, and with that change his descent as an artist was startlingly rapid.

The extent and speed of his loss of reputation may be gauged by the sharp change of attitude toward him by other writers. Early in 1921, Paul Rosenfeld invited Sherwood and Tennessee on a trip to Paris and London at Rosenfeld's expense. The Andersons eagerly accepted the invitation; and when Anderson arrived in Europe, he discovered that he was widely respected. Shortly after arriving, he called on Gertrude Stein at 27 rue de Fleurus; and while Anderson gallantly acknowledged her influence on his style, it was she who expressed the gratitude of the unacknowledged writer for the encouragement from the influential one. "Sherwood Anderson came," she wrote later in *The Autobiography of Alice B. Toklas,* "and quite simply and directly as is his way told [Gertrude Stein] what he thought of her work and what it meant to him. . . . He told it to her then and what was even rarer he told it in print immediately after. Gertrude Stein and Sherwood Anderson have always been the best of friends, but I do not believe even he realizes how much his visit meant to her."[22] Before the end of May, James Joyce, the author of *A Portrait of the Artist as a*

Young Man and the first sections of *Ulysses*, paid honor to Anderson's reputation by calling upon him at his hotel. In England, on the return trip, he was welcomed and entertained by the genial novelist and editor of the *English Review*, Ford Madox Ford, and he was received cordially by the venerable poet laureate John Masefield.

Though this heady European reception prompted Anderson to remark somewhat caustically in a letter from England to his brother Karl that he found his work taken more seriously in Europe than in the United States,[23] he had gained the respect of a number of brilliant younger writers. F. Scott Fitzgerald, whose *This Side of Paradise* officially opened the new Jazz Age, called him a "wonder." Ernest Hemingway, who had come to the apartment of mutual friends, the Y. K. Smiths, in Chicago to listen politely to Anderson's theories of writing, openly acknowledged his great admiration for Anderson's work and frankly declared his intention to pattern his career after Anderson's.[24] And Sinclair Lewis, whose *Main Street* (1920) had almost immediately brought its author the wide recognition Anderson aspired to, had—as Anderson wryly admitted—written favorably enough of his work to boost appreciably the sales of *Winesburg* and of *Poor White*.

By 1926 his great reputation was under serious attack. The most serious blast came from Hemingway, whose *Torrents of Spring* was a devastating parody of *Dark Laughter*—among other things. Whatever Hemingway's motives (it is clear that while he personally disliked Anderson, he nevertheless identified with painful accuracy the precise nature of the affectation of *Dark Laughter*), *Torrents of Spring* was at once a culmination and an epitome of the dissident critical opinion that began with the appearance of *Many Marriages* and that grew loud after the publication of *Dark Laughter*.

IV *The Social Critic*

By 1927, Anderson seemed to be a writer with nothing to say, and he struggled in vain for the next three years to rejuvenate the imaginative powers he knew he had lost. He adopted a new role which, he hoped, would enable him to renew his contacts with the simple small town folk about whom he had done his best writing. He felt that fame and success had separated him from people. "There is always the chance.... of the separation [from] life of the professional writer," he told Marco Morrow in December, 1927. "A man becomes famous. . . . It only means you become a public character, and who wants that? I hold to the opinion that writing should be an incidental part of life, not the leading thing in life. If you acquire fame, people begin putting you outside themselves."[25] He decided, like Bruce Dudley in *Dark Laughter*, to leave the sophisticated life of the big city and to return to the simplicity of the small town. Convinced that fame had destroyed him, he deliberately shaped for himself the part of obscure small-town editor and country gentleman.

In the summer of 1925, he and his third wife—Elizabeth Prall, whom he had married in 1924—had stopped en route to New Orleans in Sugar Grove, Virginia, a hamlet a few miles south of Marion. He found the area pleasant and the hill people to his liking. "The hill people are sweet," he wrote to Alfred Stieglitz. "No books, little false education, real humbleness. It does so beat talking to pretentious half-artists. We may try to acquire a few acres and a cabin."[26] The next year he returned with Elizabeth to Virginia, where he bought a farm near Marion, and in 1927, after another trip to Europe, he built a large stone house near Ripshin Creek which was to be his home for the remainder of his life. With money borrowed from Burton Emmett, he bought the two Marion weekly newspapers, the *Democrat* and the Republican *Smyth County News*, which he allowed to retain their separate political identities, while he wrote homely, chatty sketches in the manner of a rustic "Poor Richard" or of a "Spectator." He published these sketches in 1929 as *Hello Towns*. He expected the newspapers to provide him with a regular income that would relieve him permanently of recurrent financial problems. Operating them and writing his weekly columns would give him something to do "out of necessity" and also put him in daily contact with the hill people and townsfolk.

But while the quiet life of the mountain town helped reduce the pressures of fame and brought him the anonymity he wanted, Anderson was not long satisfied to remain a small-town editor and a country gentlemen. Since he traveled infrequently, he soon felt his isolation from the literary milieu he had known in New York and in Chicago. Despite his claim that he and Elizabeth were "both leading much healthier and saner lives" in Marion, he did not readily find the revitalization of his imaginative powers he had thought the simpler life in the Virginia hills would bring him. For a time he enjoyed operating and writing for his two weeklies, but he was ready by 1929 to turn them over to his son Robert. Finally, in January, 1929, his third marriage ended in divorce, and in June he wrote to Ferdinand and Clara Schevill: "To tell the truth, I have been this year more dispirited than I ever remember to have been. That made me determined to throw everything up and try something new, as I had done so often before—a new place, a new woman, a new book, etc."[27]

Discouraged by the disintegration of his marriage and by his inability to regain his imaginative vitality at Ripshin, he went to Chicago in December, breaking at last from what had amounted to a kind of voluntary exile from twentieth-century life. He was writing *Beyond Desire* (1932), and he was in desperate need of the assurance success would bring. "I think you know, Horace," he wrote to Liveright, his publisher, "that I have to get this book right, not only on account of its chances of success, but also because of myself. I want to whip out of me this sense of defeat I have had."[28] Once more, the course of his own life was foreshadowed by the role assumed by one of his heroes; like Red Oliver in *Beyond Desire*, he emerged from the village to champion the cause of the working man, becoming a reformer—a role he was to maintain for the rest of his life.

In 1930 he met and fell in love with Eleanor Copenhaver of Marion; and, while it was two years before they married (it was Anderson's last and most happy marriage), the socially conscious Eleanor helped concentrate his interests and to direct them into action. Soon he was observing firsthand the conditions in the mills of the Southern small towns and enlisting aid for the cause of the workers. By mid-1930, he was able to write to the Schevills: "I do seem to myself alive again and wish you could see me now, rather than have the memory of me as I was last winter . . . I did right to go to the factories. I'm going back to them this winter."[29] In September he was involved in the strike at Danville, Virginia; and he wrote to such notables as Clarence Darrow for support of the workers. The Communists were active in the strike; but, while he admired them for taking effective action in behalf of labor and at various times during the next decade gave his name in support of their efforts,[30] he never became more than their ally in the cause of labor and he never adopted theoretical Marxism—being, as always, opposed to doctrines for human conduct and destiny. It was the "new gods—money power, imperialism, industrialism" he despised, not merely the capitalistic control of them; and his concern was for humanizing rather than communizing the social system.

In *Perhaps Women* (1931), a book of essays on his impressions of life in the factories, he put forth the proposition that the machine has taken from men the creative function they enjoyed as craftsmen, rendered them sexually impotent and spiritually empty, and robbed them of both freedom and dignity. It is scarcely to be wondered at that, believing himself to have been "saved" by a woman, Anderson could with some self-assurance predict to Charles Bockler that "we will have to turn to women so, crying, Save us. Save us. We cannot save ourselves."[31] In his last full-length narrative, *Kit Brandon* (1936), he portrayed the strange loss of maleness in modern men and the noble efforts of women—themselves compelled to assume the masculine traits surrendered by men—to combat the effects of the machine.

But behind his hopes that women could salvage humanity in the machine age lay the same primitivistic agrarian moral assumptions he had always held. Kit Brandon never rids herself of the effects of the machine, but she learns that the source of genuine fulfillment lies in the simple agrarian values of the past as she secretly observes a young farmer and his wife enjoying the vigorously sensuous, happy life close to the soil;

working together in their common cause on the farm; and ful-
filling their lives in each other and in the land. Nowhere in
Kit Brandon is there any suggestion that the corrupt political
and economic system Anderson portrays in his microcosm ought
to be changed by legislation. In his final role as radical and
social critic, Anderson repeatedly put forth—as he does in *Kit
Brandon*—psychological and moral rather than political or economic solutions to the problems of the machine age. In all the
roles he had assumed, he was basically a moralist; and to the end
of his life he regarded the invasion of the great American continent by the factory and machine, and the growing absorption
of the child-like American with gadgets and profits, as results of
negligence of the sacred human responsibility toward nature
and one's fellow man.

In his final work, the posthumously published *Memoirs,* he
asked rhetorically in a letter addressed to Mrs. Copenhaver,
his mother-in-law, "where in the world can be found more beautifully sensuous hills [than in Virginia]? . . . food being raised
for people to eat, wheat waving in summer winds, the curious
majesty of growing corn. How does it happen that money
can buy or sell such acres?"[32] Thoreau had asked the same
question a hundred years before; and, like Thoreau, Anderson
refused to accept the idea that money and machines could
make life better. He believed with Thoreau that the great
mass of men lived lives of quiet desperation in what he called
their "terrible loneliness," and nothing short of a complete psychic and moral rebirth could save them. "I . . . . think that the real
war coming is not . . . between Communism and capitalism," he
told Dreiser in 1935, "but between this obsession with fact and
the other conception of in some way recreating a pathway between men."[33]

During the final decade of his life he assiduously sought—not
always successfully—to re-create a pathway between himself and
others. Besides *Perhaps Women, Kit Brandon,* and the *Memoirs,*
he wrote journalistic sketches and essays about individuals in
the villages and about the problems of small-town America
which he gathered and published in *No Swank* (1934), *Puzzled
America* (1935), and *Home Town* (1940). In none of these

works of his last ten years did he regain the power of that brief period of greatness he enjoyed from 1914 to 1922; but in moving sympathetically into the inner lives of the rural and factory folk, he tried hard to live as he believed men must if life is to have any value. When he died in Colon, Panama Canal Zone, on March 8, 1941, he was en route to South America as a kind of unofficial literary ambassador of good will for the State Department. He had arranged with the *Reader's Digest* to do a number of articles on the "little" people of South America, and he was interested, characteristically, in "getting to understand a little their way of thinking and feeling, and trying to pick up the little comedies and tragedies of their lives."[34]

CHAPTER 2

The Populist Temper

WHEN HE WAS WRITING the autobiographical *A Story Teller's Story* in August, 1923, Anderson wrote to Van Wyck Brooks that he was "frankly daring to proclaim" himself "the American Man." "I mean by that," he told Brooks, "to take all into myself if I can—the salesman, businessman, foxy fellows, laborers, all among whom I have lived. I do get the feeling that I, in a peculiar way and because of the accident of my position in letters, am a kind of composite essence of it all."[1] Well before 1923, he had transformed the main configurations of his own life into the psychological and moral metaphor that formed the thematic and structural framework of all his novels. His remark to Brooks was merely an open acknowledgment that he now consciously regarded the principal features of his life as a kind of summation of the essential American experience. Though *Windy McPherson's Son* and *Marching Men* are frequently stilted in diction and represent the work of a talented businessman rather than an accomplished artist, they reveal the nature of that metaphor and the moral and social ambiguities that helped shape the chief, significant contours of Anderson's work.

In both books we follow the heroes, Sam McPherson and Beaut McGregor, as they move (much as Anderson himself did) through three successive stages toward maturity and moral consciousness: the youth spent in a small town, the escape to the city and pursuit of success, and the sudden abandonment of the success ethic. Unlike Anderson himself, whose break with convention was clearly a case of psychic necessity, McPherson and McGregor repudiate the individualistic values of a materialistic society for moral reasons; but, whereas Anderson's struggle was primarily one for psychological wholeness, theirs represent moral journeys first to consciousness and then to conscience.

Showing a moral strength Anderson himself could not muster, Sam and Beaut become reformers. Though the nature of their reform efforts differs, they have in common the rise from the spiritual and material poverty of their small-town youth to almost Napoleonic power as men of the people. McPherson, who becomes a business tycoon, plays the role of the "inspired millionaire," a kind of Frank Cowperwood who suddenly becomes conscience stricken. McPherson abandons the Darwinian world of business and throws his great personal strength into helping oppressed farm and factory workers in their conflicts against emotionally insulated capitalists, corrupt union officials, and brutal hireling managers. McGregor, who like McPherson ruthlessly tramples on those weaker than himself in his climb to success, also grows aware suddenly of his responsibilities to the exploited "little" people and organizes a mammoth Marching Men Movement in order to bring "old labour in one mass . . . before the eyes of men" and to "make the world see—see and feel its bigness at last." Neither has a discernible economic or political plan of action or goal, other than the determination to help the weak become strong enough to compete on equal terms with their industrial, financial, and political oppressors; and both fail in their reform efforts, though Anderson lets us believe they have achieved moral victories in making the effort.

Like Dreiser, Anderson presents a Naturalistic picture of people caught up in social "forces"—specifically, by a repressive, individualistic economic system and by an outworn Puritan morality which have defeated the weak and made egoistic monsters of the strong. But, unlike Dreiser, Anderson judges society against an ambivalent nature in which man may choose between harmony and discord, between a moral order based upon concord and a chaotic social system grounded in egoistic competitiveness. Though they "fall" into egoism and accept the community's ethics of competition, both of his strong men have an innate moral conscience which is not—as it is in Dreiser's

Cowperwood—merely a social contrivance. Whereas Cowperwood struggles for survival in a Darwinian world that reflects a warring, amoral nature, Anderson's heroes fight their way to power and success in a society that has lost touch with a benevolent and harmonious nature and become egocentric. Anderson departs further from the traditional Zolaesque and Dreiserian reductive Naturalism in providing his heroes with a choice between a nature of strife on the one hand and a nature of harmony on the other—between an egoistic, competitive life and one of sympathetic communion with others. During the course of his search for "truth" after abandoning the world of big business, McPherson one day observes the random fighting of two guinea hens:

> Again and again they sprang into the fray, striking out with bills and spurs. Becoming exhausted, they fell to picking and scratching among the rubbish in the yard, and when they had a little recovered renewed the struggle. For an hour Sam had looked at the scene, letting his eyes wander from the river to the grey sky and to the factory belching forth its black smoke. He had thought that the two feebly struggling fowls, immersed in their pointless struggle in the midst of such mighty force, epitomized much of man's struggle in the world. . . .

The background of factories clearly identifies modern, urban, industrial society and a decayed agrarian culture with a nature of brute conflict. But, in contrast to Dreiser's Cowperwood, who accepts a predatory human existence as a reflection of nature (recall, for instance, the famous scene in *The Financier* in which he observes a lobster devour a squid and concludes that that is the "way things are"), Anderson's McPherson charges the American people with moral responsibility for their failure to live in harmony with a benevolent nature. "American men and women," he declares, "have not learned to be clean and noble and natural like their wide clean plains." McGregor also makes a moral indictment as he rejects the idea of progress and contrasts a harmonious nature with American society: "Orators might have preached to him all day about the progress of mankind in America, flags might have been flapped and newspapers might have dinned the wonders of his country into his brain. He did not know the whole story of how men, coming out of Europe and given millions of square miles of black fertile land [,] mines and forests, have produced out of the stately order of nature only the sordid disorder of man." The economic struggle thus for Anderson becomes a psychological struggle, and the social conflict, moral; and, where Dreiser's naturalism is of the "scientific" variety that owes its origins to Zola, Anderson's is romantic and derives from indigenous sources, as we shall see.

Achievement of maturity for McPherson and McGregor comes when their innate need for order and communion becomes a conscious moral imperative; when aware of their share of their country's guilt, they rise to what Anderson later called—in reference to Twain—a "proud conscious innocence."[2] Both books are thus primarily psychological and moral in theme rather than political or economic, and we see in them the basic moral assumptions that are implicit in such later works as *Winesburg, Ohio.* McGregor and McPherson reject socialism as an alternative to an oppressive capitalistic system. In contrast to such contemporary heroes as Jack London's Ernest Everhard in *Iron Heel,* Anderson's two strong men are moral rather than utopian socialist leaders; the pattern of development they follow is one that takes them to social consciousness and conscience rather than to economic or political theory. Their sudden abandonment of the pursuit of their own self-interest represents a return to the community of oppressed, defeated people they have rejected and also a moral acknowledgment of social responsibility.

As Anderson's heroes move from the small towns to the larger world of Chicago and come into conflict with society on all levels, they follow the traditional pattern of one of the most common American literary heroes, the "American Adam." That pattern in its broadest outlines consists of what R. W. B. Lewis has termed "the ritualistic trials of the young innocent, liberated from family and social history or bereft of them; advancing hopefully into a complex world he knows not of, radically affecting that world and radically affected by it; defeated, perhaps even destroyed.... but leaving his mark upon the world, and a sign in which conquest may later become possible for the survivors."[3] Both McPherson and McGregor are initially innocent in the sense that they instinctively want to "draw close" to others in harmonious human relationships; but, repelled by the disorder and ugliness of their respective communities, they repudiate their hometowns, and in doing so, they undergo a "fortunate fall" into the very isolating egoism that causes the ugliness and disorder they have tried to escape. Thus, though isolated, they share the guilt of society, and their awareness of that guilt and their determination to atone for it comprise a symbolic moral rebirth—that is, the achievement of a "wise" innocence, now armed by experience and grounded upon understanding of its own ineradicable sense of guilt.[4]

As Lewis has well demonstrated, the myth of the American Adam is one of the more substantial in American literature; it finds expression notably in Thoreau's *Walden* and Whitman's *Leaves of Grass* and in works of Cooper, Hawthorne, Melville, James, Twain, Hemingway, Faulkner, and others. Variations on the theme are as numerous as the writers who have—consciously or unconsciously—used it; but it is most commonly expressed in terms of a moral journey, a loss of innocence and an effort to regain it. Lewis characterizes the Adamic narrative metaphor as "the birth of the innocent, the foray into the unknown world, the collision with that world, the 'fortunate fall,' the wisdom and the maturity which suffering produced."[5] Cooper's Natty Bumppo is the prototype of the innocent who shuns society for the innocence and purity of life in the wilderness; Hawthorne's Donatello and Miriam in the *Marble Faun* are innocents who fall prey to evil because they are unequipped by experience to cope with it, as do Melville's Billy Budd and such Jamesian protagonists as Christopher Newman, Adam Verver, Milly Theale, and Isabel Archer. And Mark Twain's Huck Finn defines his essentially innocent nature in acting against his socially developed conscience to help his friend Jim escape from slavery.

In the twentieth century the metaphor has become transfigured. The Adamic hero carries, from early in life, the burden of society's guilt; and, often in response to moral or psychic necessity, he embarks upon a quest for primal Edenic innocence and purity, a quest which culminates in psychic purification or moral rebirth through an elaborate ritual that renews his sentient and psychological contact with nature. Hemingway's Nick Adams and Faulkner's Ike McCaslin (in "The Bear") are among the most notable contemporary Adams who attempt to find a kind of primitive psychic innocence by means of a ritual contest (fishing and hunting, respectively) between themselves and nature.

Anderson's heroes follow a course in which they first fall prey to the corrupting effects of a materialistic and traditionally moralistic society; but then, as they become conscious of their "fall," they reject the values of convention and deliberately seek a revitalized innocence based upon experience. Consciousness or awareness of their "fall" comes to them suddenly as a result of a growing psychological reaction against the life they are living; and, as this natural psychological revulsion turns to a sense of guilt, the conventional becomes unnatural and therefore immoral, while the innermost, natural inclinations and needs become moral. Thus McPherson strives to quell the "man of achievement" in himself which has separated him from others and to respond to his second, "buried" personality, which draws him instinctively to others and compels him to "try to understand . . . other lives, to love."

The Adamic journey became the characteristic narrative metaphor in all of Anderson's subsequent novels, assuming social and psychological as well as moral and mythical dimensions. Like McPherson and McGregor, Hugh McVey of *Poor White* (1920), John Webster of *Many Marriages* (1923), Bruce Dudley of *Dark Laughter* (1925), Red Oliver of *Beyond Desire* (1928), and Kit Brandon of *Kit Brandon* (1936) embrace variously the ethics of success; the doctrine of progress; standardized, hypocritically sexual notions of love and courtship and marriage; or the bloodless piety of Puritan morality. And like McGregor and McPherson, they all rebel against the spiritual confinements of society and try to find and live by a principle of order in the face of the social disorder they have observed everywhere and the inner disorder they have felt in themselves and seen in others. All have a strong instinctive need for order—for example, McPherson's efforts to make an "art" of business and McGregor's obsession to "bring an end to disorder" in society—which reflects the chief cause of Anderson's own psychic crisis in 1912. And all escape from the disorder of their lives and begin a new life that develops into a moral quest, a groping effort to construct a new moral world.

Such a narrative metaphor lends itself to penetrating literary examinations of a cross-section of American life. The assumptions implicit in the moral journey Anderson's heroes take are not hard to identify, for they comprise the strange amalgamation of Jeffersonian agrarian primitivism and secular Calvinism that made up the "folklore of Populism" which was—and to some extent still is—a powerful ideological force in Anderson's Midwest. A brief examination of Populism and its "folklore" explains the thematic attitudes of *Windy* and *Marching Men* and enables us to assess them on their own terms.

Historian Richard Hofstadter distinguishes five chief themes in the Populist ideology, all of which may be identified in varying degrees in *Windy McPherson's Son* and in *Marching Men*: "the idea of the golden age; the concept of natural harmonies; the dualistic version of social struggles; the conspiracy theory of history; and the doctrine of the primacy of money."[6] The first two of these themes are primitivistic, and are historical remnants of Jeffersonian agrarianism. The idea of the golden age looks backward in time and is one of the oldest forms of chronological primitivism. For the Populists, the golden age lay in the pre-industrial era of the young Republic, when the hardy yeoman farmer, uncorrupted by city-bred notions of profit, worked harmoniously—and thus virtuously—with a benevolent nature.

One of the chief historical facts about the Populist Revolt is that it signified a shift in agrarian attitudes from hope for an agricultural Eden in the future to memory of an imagined golden age of the past. The agrarian myth, which had drawn settlers westward throughout the nineteenth century in search of a new Eden, changed after the Civil War as repeated natural disasters and growing problems with land speculators, mortgagors, and railroad monopolists turned the "garden of the world" into a "desert."[7] The growing agrarian sense of cultural failure which accompanied the Industrial Revolution and which was expressed in the Populist Party platform of 1892[8] generated the conviction—seen in such other Populist writers as Masters and Lindsay—that, given an opportunity to begin life again in a new Eden, Americans had failed to build a society commensurate with the great abundance and beauty of the continent.

The "concept of natural harmonies," against which McPherson and McGregor judge the "sordid disorder" of the farms, the towns, and the industrial cities, commonly manifests itself as cultural primitivism, the conviction that life lived close to nature is wholesome and virtuous. In *Windy* and in *Marching Men* this theme is closely related to the nostalgic, agrarian Edenic myth. As youths, McPherson and McGregor respond simultaneously to the beauties of the idyllic countryside and mountain valleys. One morning when he is a boy, Beaut McGregor goes with his father to a valley over the mountain from the squalid town of Coal Creek and sees an agricultural Eden:

> On the first morning, when the boy sat on the hillside with his father, it was spring and the land was vividly green. Lambs played in the fields; birds sang their mating songs; in the air, on the earth and in the water of the flowing river it was a time of new life. Below, the flat valley of green fields was patched and spotted with brown new turned earth. The cattle walking with bowed heads, eating the sweet grass, the farmhouses with red barns, the pungent smell of the new ground, fired his mind and awoke the sleeping sense of beauty in the boy. He sat upon the log drunk with happiness that the world he lived in could be so beautiful. In his bed at night he dreamed of the valley, confounding it with the old Bible tales of the Garden of Eden, told him by his mother.

As McGregor grows to mature consciousness, the concept of natural harmonies becomes transformed into human terms, and the harmony of nature becomes the desired norm for harmonious psychological relationships—expressed by means of psychic collectivism or communion in *Marching Men*.

In the Populist ideology, the traditional primitivistic belief that society has deteriorated since the "golden age" of natural and human harmonies was charged with a latent Calvinistic moral Manicheanism which conceived a "dualistic" version of social struggles consisting of a clear-cut division between the demons of "money power, monopolies, and satanic mills" on the one hand and the simple rustic folk and workingmen on the other. Behind the evils of these Populist demons lay the lure of money, which in *Windy* brings about the "fall" of Sam McPherson. Like the manufacturer Ormsby in *Marching Men*— who was at one time an honest tradesman—Sam degenerates morally as he becomes rich; and we see him conspiring with other businessmen to manipulate the stock market and to capture control of his father-in-law's arms manufacturing company. The dualistic version of social conflicts is even clearer in Beaut McGregor's Marching Men crusade against the capitalists; and the "conspiracy theory" shows itself in the fact that the first glimmerings of social conscience come to him when he exposes a scheme by the corrupt business-controlled Chicago political machine to throw the blame for a murder upon one of its petty hirelings who is innocent.

The intellectual weaknesses inherent to the Populist folklore are obvious, and Anderson's attempts to confront complex political, social, and economic issues with psychological and moral solutions reflect the unfortunate (and dangerous) failure of the Populists to implement their moral fervor with intelligence. Unable to unite for any length of time on a political or economic program, generally unreceptive to theories of reform, and frustrated by their feeling of weakness before the great commercial powers, the Populists were responsive to the appeals of the strong-man hero of the people, the inspired political "white knight" who could articulate their grievances, marshall their diffused strength, and lead them in a crusade against a formidable—and sometimes nebulous—enemy. At times, as when they followed John Peter Altgeld, the hero who set free the men involved in the Haymarket Riots, they were fortunate enough to be led by a man of intelligence who combined vision with dedication to the cause of the "people" and personal disinterest. But they were by no means uniformly judicious or consistent in their choice of a leader; and they were often more susceptible to the blandishments of impassioned demagogues than to the articulation of a clearly defined political or economic course of action. The notion that a Napoleonic folk hero was needed was commonly held. In a biography of Napoleon published in 1902, Populist leader Thomas E. Watson saw the conquering Corsican as a "great democratic despot"; and the militant Mary E. Lease contended that "we need a Napoleon in the industrial world who, by agitation and education, will lead the people to a realizing sense of their condition and remedies."[9]

This Populist hero-worship—abetted by Anderson's reading of Carlyle and, probably, of Jack London's Nietzschean proletarian novels—surely lay behind the creation of Sam McPherson and Beaut McGregor. It is pervaded by a thinly veiled contempt for the masses with whose interests it purports to concern itself; McGregor and McPherson show a kind of Carlylean and Nietzschean scorn for the "rabble" even as they try to unite them, and both books reveal a Calvinistic concern for the secular elect, "extraordinary men" who "now . . . suffer terribly" in a democracy.

Grounded in the Populist ideology, with its political and social mindlessness, such power- and hero-worship is potentially fascistic. As Anderson later ruefully admitted, the peculiar type of collectivism drawn in *Marching Men* was effected by the fascist dictators in Italy, Germany, and Spain during the 1920's and 1930's.[10] The brand of anti-commercial sentiment seen in McPherson's "rebellion" is scarcely as far removed from the business ideology as it might appear to be, for McPherson remains a businessman-hero to the end; and we are given to believe—in a style that sometimes sounds like an advertising blurb—that he has achieved a neat, comfortable moral awakening: "He is a rich man, but his money, that he spent so many years and so much of his energy acquiring, does not mean much to him. What is true of him is true of more wealthy Americans than is commonly believed. . . . Men of courage, with strong bodies and quick brains, men who have come of a strong race, have taken up what they had thought to be the banner of life and carried it forward."

The intellectual problems implicit in confronting a corrupt and complicated modern society with an Adamic hero equipped with little more than a strong but recently gained moral conscience were to plague Anderson to the end of his career. But traces of the kind of work he was to do in *Winesburg, Ohio* are evident in these books, particularly in *Windy*; and suggestions of a more useful character type than the Adamic hero—distinguished by a perverse obsession with an innocence that violates conventional modes of behavior—appear in the early sections of both books. A number of admirable scenes involve minor characters who are beaten by life, grotesques of the villages and cities who adumbrate the twisted figures of *Winesburg* and the ones that appear in the better tales in *The Triumph of the Egg* and *Horses and Men*. In his portrayal of the abrupt initiation into their world of young McPherson and McGregor and of the painful loss of youthful detachment from the adult world, we see the combination of characters, narrative techniques, and style that brought Anderson's art to its peak of perfection.

These scenes are for the most part found in the first two sections of both books before McPherson's life "ceases to be the story of a man and becomes the story of a type, a crowd, a gang," and before McGregor becomes a proletarian organizer. These scenes are characterized by the fact that McPherson and McGregor act as centers of consciousness who absorb the life about them in the form of impressions. Though rendered objectively in a realistic, reportorial style, the best scenes are filtered through the sensitive inner lives of the heroes and dramatize both the externally observed action and the observers' feelings and thoughts. Thus, like Stephen Crane, Anderson portrays the initiation of his heroes into a complicated world by disclosing their complex responses to the world they are involved in. They grow in consciousness as they absorb the impressions everywhere of defeat and failure.

The successful fusion of Anderson's early impressionistic style with his indirectly stated themes of cultural failure and psychic defeat may best be seen when as youths McPherson and McGregor observe, with shocked and outraged innocence, the cruelty, callousness and meanness of life in the villages and in Chicago, where their fathers—the "war touched" Windy and "Cracked" McGregor—and their careworn and overburdened mothers have become human fragments; where the most intelligent and sensitive people, like the intellectual John Telfer and the school teacher Mary Underwood in *Windy,* and McGregor's father in *Marching Men,* are either tolerated as amusing eccentrics or persecuted by village gossip; and where the timid and meek are social cripples, like the generous Chicago hatmaker, Janet Eberly in *Windy,* and the shy milliner Edith Carson in *Marching Men.*

The most striking episode in either book is that in which the drunken, boastful Windy, who has persuaded himself that he was a heroic figure in the Civil War, dresses in full military regalia for the veterans' parade, mounts a splendid horse, and rides majestically to the center of town intending to open the parade with a magnificent bugle call, only to reveal—and discover—in his abortive performance that he doesn't even know how to play the bugle. In another brilliant episode, a young man named McCarthy, jailed for murder, confronts a heckling mob from his jailhouse window and jeeringly exposes the supposedly respectable women in the crowd whom he has seduced.

Such episodes as these are more common in *Windy* than in *Marching Men,* and they make it the superior work; for in those scenes Anderson's heroes are unhampered by the conscious moral purpose that turns them into the simple-minded reformers of the later sections. His best work in *Winesburg,* in *The Triumph of the Egg,* in *Horses and Men,* and in *Death in the Woods* was to be that which—as in these episodes—the frightening complexity, the puzzling contradictions, the perplexing ambiguities of the adult world first impinge upon the simple and morally ordered world of a youth and shatter his or her comfortable childhood innocence.

The form Anderson found most agreeable to that particular experience was that of the tale. With their moral legends that approach allegory and with their stylized heroes who become psychological archetypes (and thus too often lose their flesh-and-blood identity), *Windy, Marching Men* and all of Anderson's subsequent long narratives are, strictly speaking, romances rather than novels. They emphasize the subjective portrayal of heroic individuals and the growth of their inner lives and are thus to be distinguished from novels which, as Northrop Frye has usefully shown,[11] more objectively render "real" personalities in vital involvement with others in an "actual" society having the sort of balanced order and commonly accepted modes of behavior we see in the works of Jane Austen and Henry James. The tale and the short story, as Frye points out, are shorter species of the romance and the novel, respectively. It was in the tale, concerned primarily with the inner life of the individual rather than with the social relations of the group, that Anderson was to excel in writing. If he was unable to solve the problems of the individual in American society through the moral journey of his Adamic heroes in the romances, he did successfully portray in the tales that make up *Winesburg, Ohio* both the broken inner lives that characterized that society and the growth to maturity and consciousness of a Midwestern youth.

CHAPTER 3

Winesburg, Ohio

T HE IDEA OF WRITING A SERIES of thematically related sketches about individuals in a small country town initially came to Anderson from Edgar Lee Masters, whose *Spoon River Anthology* was enormously popular in 1915 and 1916; but it might just as well have come from the realistic Midwestern stories of Hamlin Garland. Proximity to Masters in time and place (Masters was also a "Chicago" writer, though Anderson did not know him) supports the likelihood that Masters' book of poems suggested the general structural arrangement of *Winesburg*. But surely Masters' work had nothing other than structural arrangement to offer Anderson, for the purposes of *Spoon River* are social criticism and satire; the essence of *Winesburg* is understanding and sympathy. Anderson found Masters' attitude toward his deceased Spoon River characters to be glib and superficial, and he felt that Masters' "successes" had been "founded on hatred."[1]

More important than Masters to the technical and stylistic qualities of *Winesburg* were the post-Impressionist painters and Gertrude Stein. Furthermore, it was during 1914 and 1915, before he had read *Spoon River,* that Anderson evolved his views of life and art which crystallized finally in *Winesburg, Ohio.*

In 1914, the famous exhibition of post-Impressionist paintings was held in the Chicago Armory, where Anderson went with Karl on afternoons to see the works of Cezanne, Van Gogh, Gauguin, and others among the "French moderns." Like such "Impressionists" as Monet, Renoir, and Degas before them, these painters portrayed the impressions of experience upon the consciousness of the artist, or of an observer with whom the artist identified himself, rather than the external appearances of events and objects. But they went even beyond the Impressionists in attempting to convey not only the subjective experience of the artist or observer but the abstract structure beneath natural forms. "You must see in nature the cylinder, the sphere, the cone," Cezanne had said. Van Gogh deliberately distorted his figures, used violent splashes of color, and swirled his brush across his canvasses to signify his own tumultuous feelings. Gauguin, the one-time stockbroker who, like Anderson abandoned business for art, drew his Tahitian natives with bold colors restrained by simple but clear lines, thereby synthesizing complex and powerful inner feelings with external forms.

Anderson's interest in painting at this time was more than casual: he himself painted. While he never seriously considered making a career of it, he painted passably enough to sell two of his canvases for $200 each, and the techniques of composition in Impressionist and post-Impressionist art—carefully explained to him by Karl, who was himself a painter of some merit—offered possibilities in form and texture for fiction that were agreeable to his own views of life and art. More specifically, the new art suggested the shaping of a narrative sequence in accordance with the flow of feelings and thoughts, or impressions, of the narrator rather than according to time: according to psychological instead of chronological time. This meant that form would develop in two ways: first, from within the narrative (as Van Gogh saw nature's form as essentially an inner thing), which required that the traditional "plot" sequence of action (Anderson particularly despised the highly plotted stories of O. Henry) would be abandoned for a form that moves with the mind and feelings; and, second, because both mind and feelings operate in a continuum of time, following moods, attitudes, or ideas rather than a chronological order, form would grow by means of a series of disconnected images which are thematically and symbolically related and coalescent like the paintings of the French impressionists. Obviously, such a narrative technique can be precarious, for the mere portrayal of random thoughts and feelings in a narrative or on a canvas is not art, which must have some sort of order. For Anderson, as for James Joyce, the new principle of order or organization was psychological rather than external and linear. The narrative counterpart to the cylinder, sphere, or cone that Cezanne saw within the complicated external disorder of nature was the epiphany, the "showing forth" of the chief significant factors, the inner reality, in the life of a character or in a situation through a symbolic act or utterance. Such is the principle of order that organizes the tales in *Winesburg*.

In an article titled "The New Note," published in the first issue of Margaret Anderson's *Little Review*, Anderson characterized the new "realistic" movement in Chicago as an attempt to regain the integrity of the old craftsman. "In the trade of writing, the so-called new note is as old as the world. Simply stated it is a cry for reinjection of truth and honesty into the craft; it is an appeal from standards set up by money-making magazines and book publishers in Europe and America to the old, sweeter standards of the craft itself; it is the voice of the new man come into a new world, proclaming his right to speak out of the body and soul of youth rather than through the bodies and souls of craftsmen who are gone."

The most significant point in this quotation is the affirmation of the integrity of the artist's feelings. In identifying the "new" artist with the old tradesman he rejected both the structural and stylistic formalization into which fiction had fallen and the objective, clinical detachment of the author from his materials such as had characterized Naturalistic fiction since Zola. Anderson called for a more subjective art which grows, as the tradesman's artifact does, out of the authentic feelings of the author and not merely out of the great accumulation of details derived from his "scientific" observations. Though he deeply admired Dreiser (who himself had broken away from the neatly plotted story) for the uncompromising honesty with which he drew his characters, Anderson moved away from Dreiser's graceless journalistic style and from his brand of stark Naturalism and surface realism in favor of techniques that permitted him to penetrate the external forces of Naturalistic fiction, to bypass the ponderous collection of external social facts, and to get to the feelings and the irrational impulses of his characters, their innermost struggles.

The style and structural techniques of Impressionism and Symbolism lent themselves admirably to these aims, and so did the stylistic practices of Gertrude Stein, whose *Tender Buttons* and *Three Lives* Anderson read at Karl's suggestion in 1914. Through her, he remarked in *A Story Teller's Story*, he gained a "new familiarity with words of my own vocabulary. I became a little conscious where I had been unconscious." He was appalled, he said, at "how little native American words had been used by American story tellers."[2] In his *Memoirs* he declared that, through Stein, he adopted the conscious stylistic intention of capturing the color and cadence of his own Midwestern speech, to lay word against word "in just a certain way" in order to convey the feelings (as distinguished from the facts) of life by means of "a kind of word color, a march of simple words, simple sentence structure."[3]

The influence of the post-Impressionists and of Gertrude Stein may best be demonstrated by perusal of "Hands," one of the best tales in *Winesburg*, in which Anderson's technique of constructing the tales around epiphanies can be seen in the portrayal of Wing Biddlebaum, whose deeply creative nature has been thwarted and perverted, through a central image of hands whose restless, bird-like activities expend themselves in random and trivial actions. The incidents of the story are clustered about this image, intensifying it and in turn being unified by it. As the incidents charge the image with meaning, the narrative proceeds to a climactic epiphany which reveals Biddlebaum's defeat to be that of the innermost self.

The narrative opens with an objective, scenically rendered paragraph showing Biddlebaum's alienation from the town and suggesting a relationship between his alienation and his "nervous little hands." It then moves in succeeding paragraphs to a generalized exposition of his more intimate acquaintance with George Willard and Willard's curiosity about the hands. Another short-view scene follows, revealing the connection between Biddlebaum's thwarted, imaginative nature and his fear of his hands. Establishment of Biddlebaum's fear shifts the narrative to a review of the events that caused him to flee from Pennsylvania to become a recluse in Winesburg. In that review we see that his hands were his means of expressing love and that the nature of this love was creative, for it found its outlet in communicating to schoolboys, through his gentle caresses, his own tendency to dream. But his caresses were interpreted as homosexuality by stupid, insensitive townspeople, and he was driven from the town. In Winesburg, he has withdrawn from the lives of others; and, unable to find creative outlet for his imaginative life, he has become a human fragment, a grotesque. The hands change from image to symbol as the narrative progresses and the themes of alienation, fear, love, and shame become in turn associated with them; and as the symbol gathers its meanings the narrative builds toward the final symbolic act, the epiphany. The epiphany occurs after Willard leaves, and the full ironic meaning of Biddlebaum's life is felt in the discrepancy between his religious posture, as he kneels, and the meaningless drumming of his fingers as they pluck bread crumbs from the floor: Biddlebaum is a kind of defeated, strangely perverted priest of love.

The narrative structure thus follows the course of the omniscient author's mind as he explores various times in the past, probes into his characters' minds, relates bits of descriptive detail, and cites scraps of dialogue—all of which add up to the final symbolic scene in which Biddlebaum's defeat is seen in the fullness of its nature. As in the best stories of Chekhov and of Crane—Anderson's Impressionistic forebear—the final scene of "Hands" is anticlimactic, for nothing happens to Biddlebaum. If the story has a "climax," it comes at the point—about half way through—in which Biddlebaum urges Willard to leave Winesburg. By deliberately violating a straight time sequence, Anderson avoids the traditional, and often artificial, plot of clear-cut cause and effect actions culminating in a decisive action, and at the same time he gains an almost tragic irony. Nothing in Biddlebaum's life can be climactic any more. His life is characterized by disillusionment, futility, and defeat; and both the anticlimactic structure and the muted tone of reminiscence support the vision of an inner life quietly but desperately submerged, and of a static, imprisoned external life.

The stasis of his life, the impasse between social repression and need for expression, can be seen in the following paragraph, in which the feeling of Biddlebaum's seething but frustrated passions is rendered by what Gertrude Stein approvingly termed "clear and passionate" sentences: sentences with simple diction and structure whose passion is conveyed by the contradictory effects of emotional balance and antithesis. We should notice how the terms *beat, action, desire, sought,* and *pounding* are subdued and counterpointed by *comfortable* and *ease*: "When he talked to George Willard, Wing Biddlebaum closed his fists and beat with them upon a table or on the walls of his house. The action made him more comfortable. If the desire to talk came to him when the two were walking in the fields, he sought out a stump or the top board of a fence and with his hands pounding busily talked with renewed ease."

Not all the tales in *Winesburg* are so felicitously constructed and executed as "Hands," but the best of them, like the book as a whole, convey the feeling of isolation, loneliness, and defeat through grotesque characters. Though the tales are self-contained and complete in themselves and may be read individually with enjoyment, they gain an added and very important dimension when read consecutively as episodes in a single narrative; for *Winesburg* as a whole presents a unified portrayal of the growth to maturity and consciousness of young George Willard, who develops as the symbol of the "whole" man against whom the grotesques stand as fragments.

Like Dickens' *David Copperfield,* Meredith's *The Egoist,* and Joyce's *Portrait of the Artist as a Young Man, Winesburg* is—in addition to being a collection of tales—a *bildungsroman,* a story of a boy growing to manhood and becoming involved in the perplexing world of adults. Though he does not appear in all the tales, Willard shares importance in the narrative with the grotesques, to whom he is the symbolic counterpoint. The most profitable approach to the book, therefore, is to examine the nature of the contrasts between Willard and the chief characters of the tales.

The basic contrasts are established in the prologue, "The Book of The Grotesque," for it sets forth in traditional prologue fashion the subject and theme of the work. The most important facts about the old writer in the tale are that he has at once accepted the fact of isolation and achieved inner wholeness through rich and sympathetic relations with others like the old carpenter who visits him and never gets his work done. He is alone and isolated in his room, and in a sense his separation from the world outside suggests the social isolation of the artist. But he is a writer who does not write, and his isolation symbolizes more broadly the essential metaphysical human condition, for he has avoided the social and psychological isolation of the grotesques, having "lived" many lives. And, in his imaginative retention and re-creation of the people he has known and understood during his lifetime, he has attained a rich inner life that distinguishes him from the psychic fragmentation of the characters who pass through his mind. Having known the grotesques intimately and having heard them express their deepest feelings, he is thus something of a priest of life whose religion is all human experience, none of which he rejects. In his acceptance of isolation as a condition of life, his absorption of the lives of others, and his imaginative control over the diffuse, complex, and evasive "truths" of life, he has turned an essentially meaningless existence into a varied, abundant, and meaningful one. He has become an artist of life.

In George Willard, Anderson presents the *making* of an artist of life. Willard wants to become a writer, but before he can do so he must serve his apprenticeship to life itself. In his development we see Anderson's implied belief that the solution to the "terrifying disorder" of life, the alternative to grotesqueness, is the kind of absorption of other lives that is seen in George and in the old man in the prologue. While the artist is the archetype of the psychologically and socially liberated person, liberation is not confined to the artist; for Willard achieves freedom before he becomes a writer, and the old writer never writes his book about the grotesques.

By contrast, the grotesques are so because for one reason or another they have (willfully or because of circumstances they cannot control) become isolated from others and thus closed off from the full range of human experience. Where the old writer has accepted isolation and opened his mind and imagination to the truth of all human experience, they have attempted to embrace a single truth to live by (often, because their alternatives are limited, they have *had* to), thereby closing off other possibilities of experience and compounding their loneliness and becoming enslaved by it. The writer himself is saved by the "young thing" inside him: his imaginative receptiveness to all human feelings.

The epilogue, "Departure," rounds out the narrative by showing young Willard leaving Winesburg, where he has learned what the old writer knows about the conditions of life, and moving on to new experiences—as he must if he is to avoid becoming grotesque by remaining in the confining atmosphere of Winesburg. As he leaves, the narrator (whom we may presume to be an older Willard) surmises that "his life there had become but a background on which to paint the dreams of his manhood," a condition opposite to that of the old writer, to whom the characters of his past have become "a long procession of figures before his eyes."

Life in Winesburg impinges upon Willard in sharp, memorable moments. The structural form of the narrative from prologue to epilogue is psychological and episodic rather than linear; the tales are built about these moments of consciousness or revelation instead of following a simple sequence of time or causality. For Willard, those moments follow a pattern of progression toward increasing consciousness as he absorbs the experiences of the grotesques. On the other hand, these symbolic moments reveal the psychic limitations, confinement, or defeat of the grotesques whose lives are in a state of arrest. The narrator emphasizes in "The Book of the Grotesque" that the grotesques are not all horrible. Joe Welling in "A Man of Ideas" is comical; Dr. Reefy, in "Paper Pills" and in "Death," is a man of insight and understanding; Louise Trunnion, in "Nobody Knows," is simply pathetic.

All, however, are characterized by various types of psychic unfulfillment or limitation owing in part to the failure of their environment to provide them with opportunities for a rich variety of experience and in part to their own inability or reluctance to accept or understand the facts of isolation and loneliness. The nature of their psychic unfulfillment is revealed in the tales by epiphanies. Their development may roughly be compared to the action of a fountain which, fixed at its base and therefore moving toward nothing, suddenly overflows—as the pressure within builds up—and shows what has remained hidden from view. Just as a fountain retains the contents that have overflowed and returns them to their source, so the briefly revealed inner lives of the grotesques return unchanged to their imprisonment or defeat.

Like Joyce's Stephen Daedelus, Willard is the nascent artist serving his apprenticeship to life; but the important fact about him is that, while he is subject to the same environmental restrictions as the grotesques, he grows toward maturity and ultimately frees himself from Winesburg, while the grotesques do not. Like McPherson and McGregor of *Windy* and of *Marching Men,* Willard is a prototype of the man who is liberated from the confinement of a narrow and oppressive environment. But he differs from those earlier heroes in that he leaves at a point in his life when he has gained an intense love for the people of the town of his birth and youth, and his departure is prompted not by rejection of the town and hope for success but by a determination to broaden the range of his imaginative experience. The form which McPherson and McGregor attempted to impose upon life from without will be achieved by Willard from within: like the old writer, he lives many lives, strives to know the many truths of those lives, and grasps the wonder and mystery of life through his receptiveness to all of it.

Willard grows from passive observer of life to active participant, from aimlessly curious boy to intensely conscious adult. He is a newspaper reporter, and he appears in the early chapters as the object of actions initiated by other people or as the recipient of their advice. In "Hands" he is the target of Wing Biddlebaum's admonition to be less influenced by the people about him, the people of Winesburg; in "Mother" he is the source of conflict between his father, who wants him to stop his adolescent dreaming and become ambitious for success, and his mother, whose own unhappy life with the conventional

Tom Willard makes her fearful that George's capacity for a rich imaginative life will be destroyed, as her own was, by the conventionality of her husband; in "The Philosopher" Dr. Parcival, a recluse tortured by guilt, commands him to write the book he himself "may never get written" on the idea that "everyone in the world is Christ and they are all crucified"; and finally, in the last of these tales, "Nobody Knows," George has his first sexual experience, which is initiated by Louise Trunnion, and his nervous effort to assure himself afterward that the affair will not be known to anyone indicates that his adolescent responsiveness to public opinion—rather than a mature understanding—still dictates his moral consciousness.

From this passiveness and limited understanding of others, Willard moves, in his next stage of development, to a more aggressive role in the incidents in which he becomes involved. With "The Thinker," he has emerged as a respected personage in Winesburg; the idea that he is some day to become a writer has been established and it has given him "a place of distinction" in the town. Nevertheless, he is still an adolescent, for we see him writing a love story as Seth Richmond comes to his room, and he directs Seth to inform Helen White that he—George—plans to fall in love with her: he feels he ought to write from experience. In "The Strength of God" and in "The Teacher" this adolescent attitude toward love and literature changes to puzzled wonderment as Kate Swift's "passionate desire to have him understand the import of life, to learn to interpret it truly and honestly" in his writing becomes confused in his mind with physical desire; as he begins to understand something of the complexity of human motives and behavior he realizes that he has "missed something" Kate Swift was trying to tell him.

From "Loneliness" to the final tale, "Departure," Willard's sensibility comes to full maturity as he develops an awareness of the complicated motives and contradictory instinctive demands in life and comes to feel compassion for its victims. As he listens to Enoch Robinson's story of diffidence and misunderstanding in "Loneliness," he feels a deep sympathy for the old man that he has not previously experienced for anyone. In

"An Awakening" he conceives an overwhelming need to find a meaning in life and to put his own life in accord with it. To the gentle Tom Foster in "Drink" he displays his maturity by being able to discriminate between conflicting attitudes, without rejecting the unpleasant ones; he is "drawn towards the pale, shaken boy as he had never before been drawn towards anyone," despite his anger with Foster for fabricating a story about making love to Helen White. At the death of Elizabeth Willard in "Death," his adolescent resentment at the inconvenience caused by his mother's death in keeping him from seeing Helen White gives way to realization of the finality of death and to consciousness of the tragic beauty his mother represented. His full awareness of life's paradoxes comes in "Sophistication," when he becomes conscious of the "limitations of life" and of "his own insignificance in the scheme of existence" while at the same time he "loves life so intensely that tears come into his eyes."

With this epiphany, which is also the climax of the book, Willard "crosses the line into manhood" as "voices outside of himself whisper a message concerning the limitations of life," and as consciousness of the condition of man's isolation and loneliness is followed by his beginning "to think of the people in the town where he had always lived with something like reverence." As he walks with Helen White, they both become aware that isolation is the essential human condition and that in a meaningless universe human feelings and emotions are of supreme importance and meaning.[4] He is now able to separate closely related and confused, overlapping feelings; to distinguish passion from compassion, for instance, which he had not been able to do earlier with Kate Swift. He does not at this point want passion to obtrude upon this moment of discovery and compassion: "He wanted to love and be loved" by Helen White, but not at that instant to "be confused by her womanhood." "'I have come to this lonely place and here is this other,' was the substance of the thing felt." Both he and Helen White discover that in that dark and lonely spot they epitomize man's isolation in the universe and his sole means of living with it.

George Willard achieves maturity when he realizes and ac-

cepts loneliness as the essential human condition and understands the value of all human suffering. Understanding comes,
paradoxically, only when he has emancipated himself from the
Winesburg influence. As he stands alone and free with Helen
White, he can understand that all men are alone with their
feelings and that only through sympathy and compassion toward
others do those feelings have any meaning; or, to put it another
way, those feelings are the only really meaningful things in
life. The grotesques are people whose instinctive desires, aspirations, and deepest emotions have no meaning because they
have no "other" who will impose a meaning upon them; thus
they are drawn to the receptive, aspiring writer Willard, who
accepts and will ultimately give meaningful expression to their
feelings, or, in the case of Dr. Reefy and George's mother, to
each other.

Those grotesques who are the most sensitive and articulate
find their desires and aspirations thwarted by a repressive con-
ventionalism that offers little opportunity for fruitful human
relationships. Included in this group are Wing Biddlebaum,
Elizabeth Willard, Dr. Parcival, Enoch Robinson, Wash Williams
of "Respectability," and Kate Swift of "The Teacher." These are
the socially defeated who have been beaten by the insensitivity
and unresponsiveness of others. Along with Louise Bentley of
"Surrender" and Alice Hindman of "Adventure," they illustrate
Dr. Parcival's assertion that "everyone in the world is Christ
and they are all crucified." These people find their deepest instinctive need for love met by callousness or indifference or
misunderstanding, and they become outcasts or spiritual recluses
in Winesburg.

In contrast to Willard, they are by nature somewhat meek
and reticent and, consequently, unable to break out of their
isolation. The most hopelessly defeated of them are those who
cannot articulate their loneliness. Louise Bentley in "Surrender,"
Seth Richmond in "The Thinker," Elmer Cowley in "Queer," and
Ray Pearson in "The Untold Lie" struggle in vain to make their
feelings understood to others. Cowley and Richmond are in-
capable of responding to the understanding they want so desperately when it is proffered: Cowley, because he lacks intelli-

gence; Richmond, because of his self-paralyzing habit of analyzing everything. Neither has enough real insight or imagination to guess that others might be as lonely as they, and their resentment about their isolation intensifies their dilemma. Cowley beats the sympathetic Willard, while Richmond destroys the romance Helen White offers him with platitudes about practical matters that he really cares nothing about.

The loneliness of the grotesques expresses itself as a "vague hunger" which many of them do not understand and therefore cannot satisfy. Often its initial stages are prompted by sexual desire, but the grotesques resist the notion that it is purely physical. They adopt eccentric modes of behavior or attitudes. Those like Dr. Reefy, Kate Swift, and Wing Biddlebaum who do understand that the hunger is for meaningful communication know that the only way of abating loneliness is through absorption in others; but they are defeated by life itself: Dr. Reefy by death, Kate Swift by the fact that there is no man of her sensibility in Winesburg, and Biddlebaum by a gentleness of nature which a crude society condemns.

In the portrayal of all these defeated people a vision of American small-town life emerges in which we see a society that has no cultural framework from which to draw common experiences; no code of manners by which to initiate, guide, and sustain meaningful relationships among individuals; no art to provide a communion of shared feeling and thought; and no established traditions by which to direct and balance their lives. They live in the midst of cultural failure.

The theme of cultural failure rises by suggestion from background images of decay and decomposition. The town is a wasteland ruled by dull, conventional people. Its religion has deteriorated into an empty moralism; its people have lost their contact with the soil. While Anderson uses his images sparingly, interweaving them subtly with narrative and dialogue, they evoke an atmosphere of desolation which impinges with crushing effect upon the lives of the grotesques; and, as the images recur, they become symbolic of a culture which, as Waldo Frank has said, has reached the final stages of deterioration. Rubbish and broken glass clutter the alleys and streets of the village.

Elizabeth Willard's room at New Willard House overlooks an alleyway in which sometimes "a picture of village life" presents itself, as she observes a continuing struggle between the local baker and a cat, in which the baker hurls "sticks, bits of broken glass, and even some tools of his trade about" while the cat crouches "behind barrels filled with torn paper and broken bottles" and swarms of flies hover overhead. To Elizabeth this seems "like a rehearsal of her own life, terrible in its vividness." The houses and public buildings offer a perspective equally bleak and depressing. Dr. Reefy's office is located off a "dark hallway filled with rubbish"; Belle Carpenter lives in a "gloomy old house" in which the "rusty tin eaves-trough had slipped from its fastenings . . . and when the wind blew it beat against the roof of a small shed, making a dismal drumming noise that sometimes persisted all through the night"; and Wing Biddlebaum's small frame house offers a view of a "half decayed veranda."

The dreary face of the town reflects its dominance by what Van Wyck Brooks called "the dry sisters of Philistia"; and, though the characters who embody convention are shadowy or fragmentary, their power over the lives of the grotesques is felt as an intangible but decisive, sinister influence. They present a background of moral decay, calculation and artifice, of a rampant egoistic individualism. George Willard's father ("Mother") and John Hardy ("Surrender") embrace the religion of success; Wash Williams' mother-in-law and Helen White's mother ("Sophistication") exploit sex with varying degrees of crudity and subtlety to draw men to their daughters. Collectively, the citizens of Winesburg torture Wing Biddlebaum with shouts of deprecation. The Hardy sisters crush the sensitive Louise Bentley with hypocritical and degrading conventional courtship rites characterized by crafty use of sex.

In such an atmosphere the grotesques typically isolate themselves in rooms as barren of joy as the town itself, emerging—often at night—to walk alone or with George Willard, in whom they confide. In the darkness or within their rooms, their secret inner lives "show forth" in an epiphany, an outburst of emotion, or in a casual, unguarded remark and reveal the full extent of their psychic defeat. Thus the full force of Alice Hindman's ("Adventure") years of loneliness and sexual frustration displays itself as she rushes naked out into the rain at night, believing that the rain "would have some creative and wonderful effect upon her body."

Like Alice Hindman, the other grotesques "show forth" moments of strange beauty. Sometimes the strangeness is comical, as it is in "A Man of Ideas," where Joe Welling's unconquerable good nature combines with his loquacity and fanatic absorption with absurd "ideas" to disarm the belligerent Tom and Edward King. At other times the strangeness is pathetic, as in "Loneliness," where Enoch Robinson's loneliness is such a powerful force in his life that it becomes a kind of demon and crushes his efforts to overcome it. At still other times the strangeness is superficially ugly, as when Dr. Reefy, whose hands are large and twisted, marries the pregnant girl who comes to him; or profoundly ugly, as when Dr. Parcival refuses to treat the little girl injured in an accident. But beauty, however distorted, wells up out of the inner lives of these people who are judged queer by the culture that made them grotesque, and even in Dr. Parcival there is a weird, perverted beauty of profound understanding of the human situation in his consciousness that emotional laceration is a condition of life.

Anderson's effort to give his social theme historical perspective in the tales concerning Jesse Bentley mar somewhat the unity of the narrative. Part I of the four-part tale traces allegorically the course of modern individualism from its Old Testament beginnings to its secularized present in relating the transformation of Jesse's religious mysticism into materialism. A man of profound spiritual disposition, Jesse early in life identifies himself with the prophets of old and regards his quest for land and power as an expression of God's will. With the passage of time, his attitude changes and he thinks of his acquisitions as proof of God's favor. The "old brutal ignorance that had in it a kind of beautiful childlike innocence" in his early years (Part I) changes after the Civil War as he, "like all men of his time," becomes "touched by the deep influences that were at work in the country during those years when modern industrialism was being born." His religious passion changes to avarice under the impact of "the most materialistic age in the history of the world, when wars would be fought without patriotism, when men would forget God and only pay attention to moral standards, when the will to power would replace the will to serve and beauty would be well-nigh forgotten in the terrible headlong rush of mankind toward the acquiring of possessions. . . ."

Aside from the fact that it violates slightly the unity of setting—the other tales take place in Winesburg; this one on a farm outside of town—"Godliness," with its brief development of broad and complex historical changes, violates the symbolic structure of the book, for the narrative of Jesse Bentley's change from prophet to capitalist conforms so much to the idea it dramatizes that it lapses into direct statement and contrived allegory. Symbolism becomes allegory when the abstract analogy that the symbols embody becomes too readily definable and the idea becomes more important than the concrete action, object or character. Such is the case in this story when, for example, Jesse's new materialistic religion becomes analogous to paganism as he attempts to sacrifice the lamb; he becomes a historical abstraction. When his grandson David fells him with a slingshot, the parallel with David and Goliath approaches incredibility.

Yet the presence of this story emphasizes the importance Anderson placed upon the social and historical factors that help shape the grotesques, and it gives dramatic expression to Anderson's conception of the egoism that lies behind the two chief social forces in American life: a repressive Puritan moralism, shorn of its relation to God, and its concomitant materialism.

The total view in *Winesburg*, then, is one of a moribund culture whose symbols are human fragments. The symbols of its ancestral past—for instance, the religion that organized and gave meaning to the inner life—are exhausted and have deteriorated into lifeless individualism and soulless materialism. Its only hope is a rebirth of humanity in love, as we see it dramatized in George Willard: of recognition of man's tragic isolation and compassion generated by that recognition. Moments of beauty occur in its most sensitive citizens, but even that beauty is unnatural and grotesque, and only when individuals free themselves from egoism and face the fact of their own isolation in the universe—as Willard does—can cultural rebirth and inner fulfillment occur.

This is the substance of Anderson's message in *Winesburg*. Anderson shied away from such broad social and metaphysical statements as these, but they nevertheless, lie embedded in the lives of the characters and give *Winesburg* a significance which transcends its attachment to a specific time and place. The point of view of the omniscient author—of the mature George Willard, recalling tenderly but with detachment of time and place his small-town youth—softens the tone; it permits the town and the grotesques to emerge as objects of compassion rather than of attack, as they are in Masters' *Spoon River* and in Lewis' *Main Street*. Tone and point of view thus effectively and almost imperceptibly become thematic in themselves—in the manner of lyric poetry.

While Anderson later wrote individual tales that are superior to the stories in *Winesburg*, he never again wrote a long work that combines with such felicity the penetrating insights into the impoverished inner lives of broken, sensitive people; the sustained, pervasive mood of social degeneration; and the quiet, unforced portrayal of a hero liberating himself from the confines of his limited environment as *Winesburg* does. It is his most complete and authentic plea for freedom of expression of the inner life and for sympathetic receptivity to the needs of the human heart. Written at the dawn of an era of revolt against American provincialism and against the romanticized stories of idyllic and virtuous village life, it has outlasted both the nostalgic, sentimental romances and most of the iconoclastic satires about village life written before and since, precisely because it goes well beyond both of those oversimplified extremes to acknowledge both the worth and the tragic limitations of life in the small Midwestern towns and—by easy geographical extension—of all human life.

CHAPTER 4

Poor White: Adam in History

D ESPITE THE FACT that Anderson by 1918 felt that he had proven his ability as a writer, his inability to free himself from the necessity of holding a job and to reach a sizable audience made him increasingly conscious of his plight as a serious writer in America. In his dilemma as a productive and gifted artist who was neither widely recognized nor free from pressing financial problems, he could readily identify his own situation with that which Van Wyck Brooks claimed was epitomized by Mark Twain, whom Brooks saw as the archetype of the American artist besieged and defeated at last by the philistine enticements of money, respectability, and popular approval.

Between what Brooks called the "highbrow," the sheltered Eastern genteel intellectual who still governed American letters, and the "lowbrow," the businessman whose world of practical affairs Anderson had abandoned in sickness and despair, lay a great cultural chasm in which, according to Brooks, America consigned its brightest literary talents, those writers involved in both the intellectual and the practical life but unable to bring the two together. It was not difficult for Anderson to find in Brooks's comment that those highbrow American writers "who have possessed a vivid social talent have been unable to develop their personalities" confirmation for his own long-standing conviction that the socially talented but insulated New England Brahmins (including that expatriated Ohioan, Howells) had never touched the real currents of conflict in America. And it is by no means merely a matter of conjecture that he considered Brooks's assertion that "those of our writers who have possessed a vivid personal talent have been paralyzed by the want of a social background" painfully applicable to himself.

Brooks's most important contribution to Anderson at this time was to help him clarify his own situation as a Midwesterner and as a writer "paralyzed by want of a social background" and then to transform that lack of background into the materials of literature. In May, 1918, Anderson wrote to Brooks: "When I talked to Waldo [Frank] out here, I felt in him a sense of background I have never had. I wondered if he knew the utter lack of background. It means so very much that you know, and of course he must know also."[1] There is no reason to doubt his sincerity when two years later he exclaimed in a letter to Brooks: "if you but knew what your own clear mind has meant to me these last two or three years. Well, there's no use trying to tell you."[2] While Anderson did not of course gain his much-desired "background" from Brooks, their regular correspondence and his own preoccupation with the issues and subjects of Brooks's *America's Coming-of-Age* (1915), *Letters and Leadership* (1918), and *The Ordeal of Mark Twain* (1920) enabled him to work out the themes and symbols he needed in order to put his small-town grotesques and his Adam-hero into the stream of history.

"When you get at your Mark Twain," he advised Brooks by letter in late December, 1918, "you must do a chapter on the American going East into that tired, thin New England atmosphere and being conquered by its feminine force."[3] It is hardly coincidental that in the same letter he announced that his new book, *Poor White*, was "about laid by," for the influence of Twain in that book is palpable. Twain and Lincoln were peculiarly significant to Anderson because he saw them as boys like himself with little "background" who had left the simple rural atmosphere of the Midwest and become involved in the complicated life of Hartford and Washington, D. C., where they met perplexing admixtures of political idealism and economic self-interest, crass commercialism and genuine cultural refinement. Lincoln, he believed, had been less tainted than Twain by the evils they had confronted; but, of the two men, Twain interested him more. In his letters he referred repeatedly

to Twain's lost innocence, to the commercialism and genteel
cultural elegance that came dangerously close to corrupting
Twain and which destroyed his youthful optimistic spirit. "The
cultural fellows got hold of Mark," he declared to Brooks. "They
couldn't hold him. He was too big and strong. . . . But their
words got into his mind. In his effort to get out beyond that he
became a pessimist." He maintained that when Twain wrote
Huck Finn, however, he had written out of his Midwestern
innocence: "He forgot Howells and the good wife and everyone. Again he was the half-savage, tender, god-worshiping,
believing boy. He had proud, conscious innocence."[4]

Though Anderson oversimplified Twain's life, the older
author symbolized for him the classic struggle of the innocent
to retain his integrity in a morally ambiguous society. For Walt
Whitman, another innocent whom Brooks held in especially
high regard, Anderson had only a limited respect, seeing—
probably with more insight than Brooks—in the flatulent disin-
genuousness of Whitman's "barbaric yawp" at its worst, an
egregious falseness neither Lincoln nor Twain was ever guilty
of. He wrote to Brooks:

> I get a sense of three very honest boys brought suddenly to
> face the complex and intricate world. There is a stare in their
> eyes. They are puzzled and confused. You will be inclined to
> think Whitman the greater [sic] man perhaps. He came closer to
> understanding. He lacked Lincoln's very great honesty of soul.
> Twain's way lies somewhere between the road taken by the
> other two men.
> I am struck with the thought that I would like to have you
> believe that Twain's cheapness was not really a part of him.
> It was a thing out of the civilization in which he lived that
> crept [in] and invaded him.[5]

The bewilderment of the innocent, the adolescent or naïve,
childlike adult as he comes into contact with the complex inter-
mixtures of good and evil, beauty and ugliness, necessity and
chance; and the puzzling mysteries of nature and the ambiguities and self-contradictions in human beings—these were
to be the themes that dominated Anderson's work from 1917
to 1922. These themes had already been central to *Winesburg*

and marginal in *Windy* and in *Marching Men;* but in Anderson's
best work between *Winesburg* and *Many Marriages* they were
enriched by a more complicated social vision, a deeper psychological penetration, and a more certain mastery of craft—a
result of his absorption, along with Brooks, in Twain as a
person and as a master of colloquial American style.

Hugh McVey, the chief character of *Poor White,* physically
resembles Lincoln (he is tall and gaunt and has a deeply
furrowed face); and he is a river boy like Twain's Huck Finn
who goes "East" (to Ohio) and becomes involved in the transition of a Midwestern town from a sleepy, agricultural village
to an industrial city. Like the heroes of *Windy, Marching Men,*
and *Winesburg,* he is an innocent who is drawn from the drab
small-town life of his youth to the enticing "city," with its
promise of a better life. But the society in which Hugh McVey
becomes entangled has a historical dimension and a pattern
of conflict that none of the communities in Anderson's previous
novels had; and, in McVey's growth to understanding of that
society, Anderson gives his most convincing portrayal of America's coming-of-age.

Poor White has, in fact, three main "characters": Hugh Mc-
Vey, Clara Butterworth, and the town of Bidwell, Ohio. During
the course of the narrative, the town moves through the historical transition from an agrarian village to an industrial city,
while Hugh McVey and Clara Butterworth develop into successively higher stages of psychic and moral consciousness. In
Hugh McVey we see the Adamic hero moving upward from an
unconscious, almost animalistic, natural innocence to an involvement in a burgeoning industrial center—wherein his innocence is lost as he becomes a party to the creation of a social
class system—and finally to realization of his own guilt and
separation from the social struggle.

Like Huck Finn, Hugh is the son of a Mississippi River loafer;
and during his boyhood he spends his time dreaming beside
the river. Though he is dissatisfied with the squalid, torpid life
of his "poor white" background, he is unable to raise himself
above the level of his father until, at the age of fourteen, he
goes to work in a railway station at Mudcat Landing, Missouri,

and is befriended by the manager, Henry Shepard, who takes him into his home to live. Shepard's wife Sarah, a practical, ambitious Yankee from Michigan, raises the stolid Hugh out of his diffused, undirected natural state and begins to civilize him. Her Yankee Puritan brand of training has two effects upon Hugh: by fixing his attention upon practical matters, Sarah sets his hitherto inactive mind in motion and directs his efforts toward understanding nature in order to conquer it; but this has a weakening effect on Hugh's inherent poetic desire to live in accord with nature. Early in life, Hugh sees nature as both destructive and benevolent; Sarah Shepard's Eastern materialism raises him to a stage of civilization above his raw natural stage and helps equip him to master and use nature.

It is that elementary stage of psychological development that he takes to the Ohio town of Bidwell after he leaves Mudcat Landing. Intensely lonely, shy and inhibited, and prevented from drawing close to other people by an "inferiority complex" (which Anderson maintained Twain had), he takes the faint beginnings of knowledge and Yankee ambition Sarah instilled in him, and, after wandering from town to town in a desperate but futile effort to enter into the lives of others, finds a job in the railway station at Bidwell. In his loneliness and isolation he turns his mind to solving trivial problems in arithmetic and tinkering with gadgets, pastimes that lead him to the invention of labor-saving farm machines.

Though he has been influenced by the Puritan Sarah Shepard, Hugh maintains his essential innocence of her exhortations to "get on" in the world, but he is motivated by a profound need to draw close to people, to penetrate the psychological "wall" that an individualistic culture has erected between persons. But his pre-experience innocence is vulnerable, like Sam McPherson's and Beaut McGregor's; he falls prey to the egoism of Bidwell's young industrial entrepreneur, Steve Hunter, because Hugh is not able to distinguish between the benefits his inventions bring to overburdened farmers and the oppression Hunter's manufacturing firm brings to the ordinary people of Bidwell. The naïve Hugh thinks that, because his motives are good, the effects of his inventions must be good. His first invention, a cabbage planter he has contrived after observing the back-breaking efforts of a farm family to plant cabbage shoots, is easily turned into a money-making enterprise by the egotistical young Hunter, who persuades Hugh to sign a contract which gives Hunter commercial control of the machine.

Though this first invention ultimately fails, Hugh continues stolidly to concoct labor-saving gadgets in the belief that they will lighten the burdens of the farmer. He is totally unaware of the paradoxical fact that, while they do help the farmer, they simultaneously destroy the individualistic agrarian culture and turn the formerly quiet and classless Bidwell into a frenetic industrial city with a new class system. After inventing a successful corn-cutter, he becomes a hero to the townspeople and at last gains self-confidence enough to become, at least publicly, a part of their lives. His newly acquired self-assurance—based largely upon the vanity of being a celebrity—is suddenly shattered when he hears a group of workingmen curse Steve Hunter and himself. He then realizes that his machines have helped create a class system of industrial barons and proletarians, that former farm boys are now embittered factory hands living in the squalor of Bidwell's spreading slums, and that his machines have actually driven people apart and generated conflict rather than lightening their burdens and bringing them together.

With the crushing of his budding self-assurance, Hugh begins at last to awaken to imaginative consciousness. Confused by the complexity of life and disillusioned with his naïve belief that technological progress means social improvement, he begins a slow journey to conscious innocence which culminates in his deliberate separation from the industrial life of Bidwell, his gradual understanding of the evil that Hunter represents, his broader sympathy for those defeated by the new industrial age, and, finally, his renewed responsiveness to beauty—buried since his "education" by Sarah Shepard but now emerging as a consciously articulated need.

Hugh's slow rise to moral, social, and esthetic consciousness represents his "coming-of-age": his liberation from absorption in "things" and his concentration upon purely human needs. His achievement of conscious innocence and maturity comes through Clara Butterworth, who undergoes her own moral journey and points the way for Hugh. Whereas the first woman in his life, Sarah Shepard, raised him out of his animal sloth, the second woman—Clara—rescues him from his spiritually debilitating career as an inventor and leads him to human fulfillment. From the moment that her girlhood innocence is outraged by an attempted assault by a young farmhand, to the time when, pregnant with Hugh's second child, she defends Hugh from a maddened tradesman, Clara develops into a woman possessed with the intuitive wisdom of the female, striving always to achieve the integrity of her instincts and desire for natural, beautiful human relationships, and fighting against repression or perversion of the sex impulse.

Reacting intuitively against the greed and vulgarity of her father, Tom Butterworth; against Steve Hunter, who represents the impotence and sterility of the industrial age; and against Puritan moral restrictions, Clara embodies the psychological norm against whom the grotesqueness of the other characters is measured. After an absurd first week of marriage, during which Hugh is afraid to come near her, she slowly brings Hugh to the fulfillment of his natural masculine role, both physically and psychologically: to realization of both his sexual desires and his need for human connection in sympathy and understanding. In her presence Hugh at last reaches the maturity of manhood, abandons his role as a maker of machines, and begins to assess his life and the society in which he lives in the broader context of humane values. He and Clara do not find satisfaction in their lives, but Anderson clearly affirms that they have at least freed themselves from the social and psychological confinements of the new industrial society, and they see hope for the future in their unborn baby.

The story of Clara Butterworth, it must be admitted, breaks the narrative into two parts and arrests the growing intensity of Hugh's involvement in the turmoil in Bidwell that is developed in books 1 and 2. Nor are the breach in unity and the shifts in emphasis from Hugh to Clara the only weaknesses that come in Book 3. The novel as a whole is heavy with summary narrative; and, while the first two sections involving Hugh and the rise of industrialism in Bidwell maintain a balance between "long view" and scenic presentation, the remainder of the novel is overburdened by statements and assertions that lack dramatic enactment. For this reason Clara remains a shadowy figure whose inner responses to the incidents she is engaged in do not generally find concrete expression in action or dialogue. To a somewhat lesser extent the character of Hugh is also presented by statements about him; after Book 2 consciousness comes to him slowly as a series of impressions that are vaguely assimilated and scarcely articulated.

The reason for this lack of distinctness can be partly accounted for by the fact that they are isolated and cut off from life; yet, when one considers how Norris, for instance, demonstrates through dramatic incidents the loneliness of his three heroes in *The Octopus,* it is readily apparent that Anderson misses the mark. The following passage illustrates the vague inner ruminations characteristic of Hugh and Clara in their growing efforts to break out of their isolation: "Like her father, Hugh seemed to Clara absorbed in only the things outside himself, the outer crust of life. He was like and yet unlike her father. She was baffled by him. There was something in the man she wanted and could not find. 'The fault must be in me,' she told herself. 'He's all right, but what's the matter with me?' "

The most admirable aspect of *Poor White* is Anderson's portrayal of Bidwell as a microcosm of the historical transition of a Midwestern town from an agricultural village to an industrial city: an Akron or Pittsburgh or Detroit. In contrast to Hugh's coming-of-age through the slow development of his physical, imaginative, and intellectual life, the town is shown moving rapidly toward disintegration. After years of struggle with the land, the people of the Middle West are ready for self-contemplation, for intellectual and esthetic development: "Men worked hard but were much in the open air and had time to think. Their minds reached out toward the solution of the mystery of existence. The schoolmaster and the country lawyer read Tom Paine's *Age of Reason* and Bellamy's *Looking Backward.* They discussed these books with their fellows. There was a feeling, ill-expressed, that America had something real and spiritual to offer the rest of the world." It is time for a cultural flowering among a people who have been compelled to carve out their own civilization and have yet to define their own heritage; but Hugh's machine comes before Bidwell is ready for it. Instead of a period of self-contemplation—which might have brought forth the thinkers, artists, and poets to give direction, beauty and expression to the new culture—Bidwell gets the factory, a class system, and vulgar, arrogant, and unscrupulous industrial barons like Hunter and Butterworth, who create a new hierarchy of wealth and power which Anderson ironically relates to that of Old Testament times.

The crushing, human price of the sudden onslaught of industrialism on the culturally crude Bidwell is shown in the violent transformations of the simple townfolk who are completely unequipped to comprehend or resist the change. The rise of the industrial class system is seen in Ed Hall, a slow-witted and harmless creature who, by the mere act of becoming a shop foreman, is placed by his friends on a higher level than themselves. The degrading effects of turning these once-independent people into unskilled wage-earners—a humiliating role they, in their naïveté, actually embrace—is symbolized by Jacob Fry, a blacksmith's son who, instead of becoming a tradesman, takes the role of a dandified hotel clerk. And the reduction of the master craftsman from proud artisan to pathetic anachronism by the shrewd operator is portrayed in the sub-plot involving the invidious manipulations of the apprentice John Gibson (who anticipates Faulkner's Flem Snopes in *The Hamlet*) to take control of the shop of harnessmaker Joe Wainsworth, who— driven finally to insane fury—kills Gibson, wounds Hunter, and attacks Hugh. The advent of public relations, the spurious myth-creation which endows the successful man with all the conventional virtues and the ideal rags-to-riches life story, may be seen in the action of Steve Hunter who, aware of the importance to business of a flattering public "image," contrives a Horatio Alger past for Hugh that fits perfectly the stereotyped ideal of the new capitalist ideology.

The episodes involving the townspeople in their own roles as townspeople—and these are not too closely tied to the theme of historical upheaval—approach at their best Twain's incisive portrayals of life along the river in *Huck Finn*. The incident, for instance, involving the baiting of Pen Beck by the blacksmith "Smokey" Fry, who is the self-appointed custodian of the town's morals, is reminiscent of that brutal scene in *Huck Finn* in which the drunken Boggs heaps insults upon the phlegmatic Colonel Sherburn and is shot and killed for it. Yet that scene and others like it in *Poor White* never quite approach Twain's episodes of river-bank society, and the chief reason is that both the irony and the dramatic immediacy of *Huck Finn* are missing from Anderson's work.

In telling his story through the innocent Huck, Twain erased himself as author from the narrative and gained the authenticity and irony of an involved central intelligence who reports the action as he has observed it; but, understanding only part of what he sees, he does not try to color or explain the significance of the action. Anderson's narrative perspective, moving in and out of the minds of his characters, summarizing and assessing historical developments, and shifting its focus from Hugh to Clara and to the various minor characters, leans too heavily upon direct assertion and too little upon scenic presentation. Twain renders the full horror of Boggs's death through the impressionable Huck—whose simple mind does nothing to violate or to color the action he sees—but Anderson relates his town episodes in terms of the subjective impressions and arbitrary judgments of the artist who is not objectified in the narrative itself. The kind of skillful handling of point of view that characterizes *Huck Finn*, whereby the naïve narrator ironically reveals more than he really understands both about society and himself, was to be for Anderson, as it was for Twain, the factor which raised his fiction into greatness. Other very special elements had, however, to be present too; and it was in a handful of short stories in which those formal, stylistic and thematic elements were fused that Anderson's art reached its peak.

CHAPTER 5

The Short Stories

THE STORIES in *The Triumph of the Egg* (1921) and in *Horses and Men* (1923) are uneven, but the best of them represent the pinnacle of Anderson's art. In general, it may be said that their quality rises in proportion to the amount and kind of ironic indirection Anderson employs in style, structure, and narrative action. The most profitable approach to them will be, therefore, to examine the means by which Anderson brings together the devices and techniques of indirection and the degrees to which he renders rather than asserts his meanings.

I *About Adults*

For convenience, the tales may be divided into two classes, those having to do with adults and those whose chief characters are adolescent boys. The "adult" stories generally have in common lonely, sensitive souls who want desperately to break out of the isolation of their inner lives. Among the best of these are the tales which are similar to the stories of Alice Hindman, Kate Swift, and Louise Bentley in *Winesburg*; tales which portray young women who are defeated by the coarseness, the insensitivity, or the moral cowardice of men and by the hypocrisy behind conventional Puritan moral codes.

The thematic key to these stories lies in the titles: "Unused," "Unlighted Lamps," "Out of Nowhere into Nothing," and "Seeds." They present a picture of waste, of human sensitivity never fully developed, of physical and spiritual potential untapped, or of a sensitive nature crushed. The pathetic May Edgely of "Unused" is the victim of Bidwell's dual standard of morality which allows the stolid Jerome Hadley to boast with impunity of his conquest of her and to degrade her in the eyes of the local gossips. Her death by drowning is an almost merciful release from life in which her longing for sympathetic companionship has brought only a mounting nightmare of terror because of the brutality of men and the sexual hypocrisy of women.

The great reservoir of love in Mary Cochran and her father in "Unlighted Lamps" is untouched, for the father fails to the end of his life to say the few simple words that would express his love—would, in fact, give it life—and make the emotional connection that could have saved them both from loneliness. Similarly, Rosalind Wescott of "Out of Nowhere into Nothing," Elsie Leander in "The New Englander," and the unnamed woman in "Seeds" are trapped within themselves and unable to satisfy the demands of their inner, imaginative lives for communication with others. The sex impulse, which could be the initial step toward breaking the barrier of loneliness that surrounds them, is reduced to an obstacle by Puritan taboos and by the animal lust these taboos set in motion.

As in *Winesburg*, Anderson develops the theme of the defeated inner life symbolically; but, where the symbols in *Winesburg* grew around repeated images of grotesqueness, those in these stories rise out of contrasting motifs of spiritual life and death, communion and isolation, light and dark. Anderson's technique of playing his motifs in a low key and in soft, muted tones, blending discordant moods, disconnected scenes and images, and antithetic themes through a kind of prose pointillism may be seen in one of the best of these tales of lonely women, "Unlighted Lamps."

This story, originally part of the novel titled *Mary Cochran* which Anderson wrote in Elyria but later revised and divided into separate tales, is constructed around the inner impressions of Mary and her father as they examine their lives in the light of his impending death, a narrative situation somewhat similar in its existential implications to Tolstoy's *Death of Ivan Ilych*. Both Mary and her father come to the painful awareness of their failure to break out of their inner isolation and to fulfill their emotional potential. The theme, suggested by the title, of an inner life failing to find outward expression rises from a series of contrasts in style, character, and scene.

The most apparent contrast is between the "buried" lives of Mary and her father and the passionate, spontaneous lives of the townspeople, particularly the immigrant laborers whose section of town Mary passes through on her walk into the country. Never having learned to respond to her impulses, Mary is drawn to the poorer district of the town "where life carried itself off darkly, with a blow and an oath"; but because of the scandal attached to her deceased mother, she cannot come close to the people of the town. She is also repelled by the crude animalism of young Duke Yetter, who misconstrues her casual gesture as an enticement.

Her father, Dr. Cochran, who has spent most of his life attending his patients without ever really entering their lives, conceals his love for Mary—as he concealed his love for his young wife before she left him—under an exterior of cool reserve. He spends his last hours before death, alone, regretfully recalling the failure of his life and resolving to "talk to the girl." "I've been a proud man and a coward," he admits to himself. As he sits alone in his dark room, sounds of a baby crying and of men talking in the livery barn across the street emphasize his isolation.

Supporting the contrasts between the doctor's buried life and the vibrant life of the town are the interrelated motifs of light and dark, of life waxing and waning, and of day fading into evening, all of which blend together, somewhat in the fashion of an impressionistic painting, to form a single impression of unfulfilled potential. The doctor's life has been lived in dimness: "It has been like a stream running always in shadows and never coming out into the sunlight," Mary observes as she watches a slow-moving stream pass along under a bridge. At the end of the story, when the doctor collapses and dies while vainly reaching out for emotional attachment, the sound of a newborn baby and the faint light of a cigarette in the dark stairway where the doctor has fallen bring together the motifs of light and dark, life and death, in ironic fusion.

Anderson's brilliant blending of counterpoints in mood, character, and theme grows almost imperceptibly by means of a shifting narrative perspective. Alternately tracing Mary's and her father's thoughts as they assess their lives, he moves back and forth across the psychological "wall" that separates Mary from her father. These shifts in point of view are abrupt, breaking off timid resolutions to act, little actions just initiated or not undertaken, scraps of life haltingly begun or left untried. The shifts and the breaks carry by indirection the idea that both main characters are afraid to follow their impulses and thus paralyze themselves with indecision.

Anderson further reinforces the theme of action begun and halted with paragraphs balanced and antithetical, such as the following: "Mary sat in the darkness by the office window and saw her father drive into the street. When his horse had been put away he did not, as was his custom, come at once up the stairway to the office, but lingered in the darkness before the barn door. Once he started to cross the street and then returned into the darkness." This paragraph begins with Mary in the darkness and ends with her father returning to the darkness. Between the first and last sentences the father makes a halting effort to leave the darkness, decides against it, and returns— an act that sums up his life, just as Mary's act of sitting apart from life in the darkness typifies hers.

The superiority of "Unlighted Lamps" over the longer "Unused" and "Out of Nowhere into Nothing" illustrates the fact that the short tale, where he deftly charged his narratives with the rich intensity of poetry, was the form most suited to Anderson's talent and materials. "Out of Nowhere . . ." is the longest piece in *The Triumph of the Egg*, running to nearly a hundred pages, and it rather tiresomely develops around the inability of Rosalind Wescott, a twenty-seven-year-old girl who has returned from Chicago to her home in Willow Springs, Iowa, to decide whether she should agree to become the mistress of Walter Sayer, her Chicago employer who is a married man. She wants to think over Sayer's proposition as a way to find "meaning" in life and to discuss it with her mother.

The most interesting person in this story is Melville Stoner,

Rosalind's neighbor in Willow Springs who is conscious that the frenetic rush of modern city life, the listless resignation to the routine of town and country life, and the dull acceptance of moral convention are but evidences of loneliness and manifestations of a thwarted inner, imaginative life. Paul Rosenfeld observed perceptively that Stoner himself is "ironically resigned to the futility of seeking to establish a permanent contact with another creature; tired to the marrow with the loneliness of existence," while Rosalind is "mortally striken in her breast by the insensitiveness and cowardice of men to whom she turns for expression."[1] In a structure built upon contrasts between death and life, night and day, shadows and light, dead trees and vibrant plant and insect life, Stoner himself is characterized by resembling alternately a vulture and a sea gull. He appears to Rosalind as death, but he actually holds out to her the promise of life through his imaginative consciousness, which struggles to free itself and needs only the response of her buried imagination. "When I was a young man and you were a girl," he tells her, "I used to sit in the house thinking of you. We've really been friends. What I mean is we've had the same thoughts."

This story also illustrates the vagueness and lack of focus Anderson's tales fall into when they have no central, unifying symbol. Lacking a controlling symbol, such tales as "The New Englander," "Unused," and this one are prolix; the narrative meanders along with foggy characters whose feelings never quite coalesce into concrete, unified thoughts. The point of "Out of Nowhere into Nothing" is that Rosalind, like Stoner, craves freedom but is trapped by the dead material facts of life that will not permit her to act in accordance with her nature. While the idea that Stoner is a caged spirit is suggested by the image of a sea gull stranded inland, no such symbol draws together the threads of Rosalind's reflections and weaves them into a unified whole. Unless woven together, the unattached images of an impressionistic presentation become random and vague. Much of Anderson's so-called "mysticism" can be written off, therefore, as a failure to grasp his vision in concrete narrative terms and a consequent tendency to make cloudy perception pass for profundity. Before she leaves for Chicago, Rosalind establishes an almost mystical "fellowship in life" with Stoner, but Anderson gives us no indication that all the impressions that have come to her since leaving Chicago have added up to anything more than a kind of aimless groping, or to any real understanding of life.

Like "Unlighted Lamps," the best tales of adult men are those in which Anderson builds his themes out of motifs that both charge and cluster themselves around a single controlling symbol, but typically the symbol is the grotesque. In "A Chicago Hamlet," the narrator relates the stories of a melancholy young advertising writer who tells of his youth on a dreary Ohio farm and of his eventual flight to Chicago where he finds the same wretchedness, meaningless activity, and tired, quarrelsome people. Pieced together by the narrator from a series of conversations in a Chicago bar, the character of Tom, the advertising writer, emerges through Anderson's technique of juxtaposing contrasting images which blend into a single impression in the reader's mind.

The most arresting incident in the story is one in which Tom, sickened by the dirty, disordered life on the farm, creeps up behind his father one night determined to kill him as the old man kneels in prayer. In this scene, Tom's sensitivity and "rather nice sense of life" disclose themselves through his compulsive, unconscious reactions against ugliness; and the struggle for purity and innocence that sums up his life is symbolized in the remarkable incident wherein Tom sees the black and yellow soles of his father's feet and returns silently to his own room where—Christlike—he washes his own feet and puts on a clean nightgown. Out of the strange juxtaposition of ugliness and beauty comes a symbolic act of grotesque innocence.

"A Chicago Hamlet" is one of Anderson's most successful Adamic stories. All the basic ingredients are present: the pilgrimage from the farm (or small town) to the big city in search of a life made beautiful by close human relationships—where people gathered "who had grown tired of loneliness and isolation"; the brief glimpses of beauty and innocence as Tom has a fleeting affair with a farmer's wife whom he "possesses" in spirit; the "fall" (in becoming an advertising writer), resulting from a paucity of alternatives and the enticements of a deceptive, commercial salvation; and finally disillusionment, defeat, and repudiation of the business ethic—in spirit if not in fact—but hope in an emergent courage and strength gained from isolated glimpses of the "fine sense of life" in others. The peculiar success of the tale can be accounted for partly by the absence of social or psychological solutions to the grotesque conditions portrayed, of which most of the other Adamic tales are not free. Moreover, Anderson achieves a felicitous fusion of fact and symbol that makes them scarcely distinguishable from one another.

"Milk Bottles," which has the same narrator as "A Chicago Hamlet," is of interest chiefly as a contrast to that tale. If, by contrast to "Unlighted Lamps," "Out of Nowhere into Nothing" lacks the concreteness, rich suggestiveness, and compression of a symbolic structure, "Milk Bottles" bears the opposite relationship to "A Chicago Hamlet." Its symbolism overpowers the flimsy factual structure of the story. In it the repeated symbol of sour milk, signifying life gone sour, descends into artificiality. And so does the main incident in which a young man who writes advertisements for a condensed milk company tastes some sour milk, writes an angry but honest story about it, but then denies the truth of his tale and returns to his spurious "masterpiece," which is, like his advertisements, a popular fabrication about happy people living contented lives.

Drawn from a thesis rather than from life, "Milk Bottles" is an example of a story in which Anderson lets his idea get away from him and control the narrative. The "idea" of the story comes through a sophisticated poet-narrator who adopts a slightly satiric tone of indulgent superiority toward the young writer's palpable and absurd lack of insight. Self-assured in his own tastes and attitudes, the poet-narrator—who clearly speaks for Anderson—betrays the same smug contempt for the bourgeoisie that Anderson despised in Mencken and in Sinclair Lewis. His contempt may be seen in his parody of the language of Babbittry: "You're all right, Ed. You're great. You've knocked out a regular soc-dolager of a masterpiece here. Why you sound as good as Henry Mencken writing about Chicago as a literary centre of America, and you've lived in Chicago and he never did. The only thing I can see you've missed is a little something about the stockyards, and you can put that in later. . . ." In such passages, the narrator is plainly toying with a stolid, superficial character; but the common-sense wisdom with which Anderson endows the narrator has its own unmistakable superficiality.

It is abundantly evident that, where he employs an urbane tone of the sophisticated narrator or of the central intelligence who understands more than he says, Anderson lapses into thematic oversimplification, cleverness, and affectation. In "The Door of the Trap" he would have us believe that Mary Cochran is "saved" from a life of failure when the college professor who acts as the central intelligence makes her aware of her sexual desires. In "The Man in the Brown Coat" the historian-narrator has written three books about the story of mankind, but he can find no words which will lead him to actual life and as a character he remains two-dimensional. The narrator in "The Triumph of a Modern" is an affected, phony artist who parlays his specious modernity into an inheritance from an "old-fashioned" aunt. When one of Anderson's sophisticated narrators speaks in first person, he typically sounds disingenuous and often gives voice to trivia, as when the narrator of "Brothers" declares, "I am sitting in my house and it rains." And, when the sophisticated, omniscient author speaks directly, as he does in "Motherhood" and "War," we get interesting essayistic narratives but not tales that bring characters to life.

The finest of the tales dealing with adult men in the two volumes are those that are related either in a groping, almost-rambling fashion by a narrator who feels rather than knows (or pretends to know) or understands, or they are told from the point of view of the puzzled, often naïve narrator (whether it be the author himself or a character) who has no preconceptions or primitivistic social or psychological panaceas. "The Other Woman" exemplifies the felicitous combination of wonder, sadness, and perplexity surrounding an incident that has revealed the complexity of life to a rather simple protagonist.

In this strange story a man tells, confessionally but without shame or remorse, of his affair with another woman on the night before his wedding and asserts that this experience helped his marriage. Although he cannot explain why he expects to be a better, more sympathetic husband as a result of the affair, it is clear that his union with the other woman has released his inner, instinctive life—hitherto inhibited by conventional moral pieties—and has helped him conquer his fear of it. Similar paradoxical discoveries contradicting conventional strictures against the authentic demands of the inner life may be seen in such admirable efforts as "The Sad Horn Blowers," "An Ohio Pagan" and "The Man's Story."

Supreme among the adult stories in both volumes is "The Egg," in which Anderson achieves perhaps the most nearly perfect blending of contrasting moods and tones, of absurdity and pathos, symbol and object, and action and theme he was ever to accomplish. Nothing in "The Egg" is extraneous to its meaning; nothing in its meaning may be extracted from the facts of the narrative. From the description of the broad swath of baldness on the father's head to the reconstruction of his ridiculous attempt to get an egg into a bottle, and from the passages relating the frustrations of chicken farming to the father's roar of exasperation at the unyielding eggshell, symbol, object, tone, mood, and diction merge in the theme of the defeat of a diffident little man by a world too complicated for him. The egg—a maddeningly fragile, refractory, and intractable thing in itself—is the symbol of those same qualities in life. The narrator's father, groping desperately for what can only be for him a precarious hold upon life as a witty and amusing rustic *bon vivant,* betrays in his efforts to place an egg in a bottle the ludicrous and pathetic chasm between his timid, hesitant nature and the recalcitrance of a perverse world of chance and circumstance. His natural diffidence will not permit him to compete on equal terms in the world of success into which his ambitious wife repeatedly thrusts him. When he tries boldly to enter that dangerous world, he so far exceeds the limitations of his nature that he becomes grotesque, at once comical and pathetic.

II *About Adolescents*

"I sang the ugliness of life, the strange beauty of life pressing in on the mind of a boy," Anderson said of the "Mid-American Chants." Such was to be the theme of his finest fiction. Sudden glimpses of the strange mixture of beauty and ugliness in life had characterized George Willard's growth to maturity in *Winesburg* and also the slow movement toward sympathetic consciousness of those defeated by the ugliness of life: Sam McPherson, Beaut McGregor, and Hugh McVey. Under the influence of Twain, Anderson brought his vision of the puzzled boy or boy-man to near perfection in a handful of tales that combine a carefully controlled point of view with a painstaking attention to the subtleties of the colloquial diction of the narrator, who betrays both a touching naïveté and a profound sensitivity to the confusing paradoxes of the adult world.

Like Huck Finn, "I Want to Know Why," "I'm a Fool," and "The Man Who Became a Woman" are related from the first-person point of view. A boy—or a man looking back upon his youth—has experienced or witnessed a baffling admixture of beauty and ugliness, purity and corruption, success and failure. The narrator himself is either unable to explain precisely what the experience means or—in the case of "I'm a Fool"—fails to understand his own role in it and misinterprets it; and, in his groping efforts to explain what he does not fully comprehend, he rambles in his narrative, feeling about for details he vaguely perceives to be significant. Typically his narrative digresses as he searches confusedly for explanations which follow his feelings rather than a logical or chronological sequence, and in his digressions he reveals the pain of entry into adult life in the perplexity he feels at seeing for the first time the ambiguities of life.

Because of his masterly handling of point of view in these tales, Anderson gains the full ironic effect of the discrepancy between what his protagonists say and what they understand or are aware of.[2] The tales may conveniently be grouped together both because their subjects consist of youthful experiences in horse racing and training and because the chief interest in each focuses upon the narrator himself. Each of the three young men is caught up in the perplexing adult world in which the simple values and beliefs of childhood are shaken by discovery that they cannot be maintained in a simple, pure form. All three cling to their youthful privilege of making absolute, categorical judgments of value; and the confusion and the perplexity they experience force them to analyze what happened in retrospect and try to relate their experience—both to themselves and to the listener-reader whom they take into their confidence—in order to understand it.

Though each of the narrators is "crazy about thoroughbred horses," horses are not the central concern of the stories;[3] the horses symbolize, variously, the simplicity of purpose and purity of sense and heart of the natural animal raised to the highest degree of perfection through breeding and training. They represent to the boys a kind of morality based upon simple response to instinct and splendid fulfillment of purpose. The boys hold a simple scale of values grounded in a hierarchy of natural purity: the stallion is more admirable than the gelding; and the swipe and the trainer, who are closer to the horses, are more praiseworthy than is the owner.

In "I Want to Know Why," the boy-narrator loses his comfortable primitivistic moral shroud as he discovers in jockey Jerry Tillford the same reaction to a prostitute that he showed toward the magnificent stallion Sunstreak, a discovery that shatters his faith in the purity of the ecstatic and almost mystical sentiment they had shared after the horse's great race that afternoon. "What did he do it for?" he asks in enraged bafflement. "I want to know why."

Up to the time he sees Jerry with the prostitute, the boy is able to keep his notions of sentiment and instinctual purity neatly separated from questions of lust and depravity. The exhilarating stimulation of the boy's senses and imagination at the track is reminiscent of the idyllic raft scenes in *Huck Finn*. Compare, for instance, these two passages, the first from Twain and the second from Anderson:

> Sometimes we'd have that whole river all to ourselves for the longest time. Yonder was the banks and the islands, across the

water; and maybe a spark — which was a candle in a cabin window; and sometimes on the water you could see a spark or two — on a raft or a scow, you know; and maybe you could hear a fiddle or a song coming over from one of them crafts. It's lovely to live on a raft. We had the sky up there, all speckled with stars, and we used to lay on our backs and look up at them. . . .

. . . .

Well, out of the stables [the horses] come and the boys are on their backs and it's lovely to be there. You hunch down on top of the fence and itch inside you. Over in the sheds the niggers giggle and sing. Bacon is being fried and coffee made. Every-thing smells lovely. Nothing smells better than coffee and manure and horses and niggers and bacon frying and pipes being smoked out of doors on a morning like that. It gets you, that's what it does.

The boy is innocent in the sense that he himself is free of taint, for he is aware of evil. He knows ugliness exists and tacitly rejects it. He knows, for instance, that the house Jerry and his companions enter is a "place for bad women to stay in"; and he is no stranger to "rotten talk, the kind a kid hears around a livery stable . . . but don't ever expect to hear talked when there are women around." What crushes and baffles him is the realization that untinged purity cannot exist in human nature, a fact which he must thenceforth live with and accept; but this knowledge destroys forever the romantic idealism of his youth. His discovery "spoils looking at horses and smelling things and hearing niggers laugh and everything." The boy's recurrent association of the horses with cleanliness and his un-complicated love for them suggest his adolescent idealization of sex. Girls are not yet much on his mind, except as disembodied ideals; and in thoroughbreds his emerging sexuality is diffused and "sublimated." "Sunstreak," he says, "is like a girl you think about sometimes but never see. He is hard all over and lovely too. When you look at his head you want to kiss him." The ex-perience with Jerry brings him later to the shocking realization that sentience can mean lust and degradation as well as response to beauty, and his initiation into the puzzling adult world in which ideals of absolute purity and beauty are impossible causes him to respond with the complete disillusionment and bewilderment of the child.

Much of the charm of "I Want to Know Why" is the result of Anderson's careful control and balance of the ironic discrepancy between what the boy consciously says and what he unconsciously reveals about himself. His chief characteristic is naïveté, and in using the naïve point of view, so splendidly used by Twain in *Huck Finn*, Anderson is able to reveal the "ugliness of life, the strange beauty of life pressing in on the mind of a boy" without resorting to direct assertion. The perspective of the naïve adolescent caught up in a puzzling conflict of values—the frustrating inability to maintain a simple, inviolate island of purity in a corrupt world—is also utilized in "I'm a Fool." In this story the chief character is a groom who, like the boy in "I Want to Know Why," comes from a middle-class family which disapproves of his connection with racing and with the "unrespectable" people associated with it. He too has an uncomplicated, uncritical love for the free, unsophisticated life among the trainers and grooms; and he also becomes initiated into the complexities of life through betrayal of his own simplicity. But whereas the other boy is betrayed by unsuspected depravity in a man he admires, this one is defeated by circumstances and by his own ignorance and inferiority complex.

The plot is simple. A young swipe relates the story of a day at the track in Sandusky, Ohio, when he left the stables and watched the races as a spectator. In the grandstands he meets Lucy Wessen, her brother Wilbur, and Wilbur's girl friend, Elinor Woodbury, from Tiffin. They immediately become friends, and, knowing which horse is likely to win, he advises Wilbur to bet on a horse that subsequently wins. Wanting more than anything else to impress Lucy, he explains that the reason he knows so much about the horse that won is that it really belongs to his father, who owns a large estate and a stable of horses which he races "anonymously" by registering the horses in the name of another man. After the races, he takes Lucy and the others to a resort outside Sandusky; and, during the course of the evening, he comes to realize that Lucy would have liked him even if he had not lied about himself and that by lying he has made it impossible to see her again. He disgustedly concludes that he is a "fool."

The plot is simple, but the meaning of the tale lies in the conflict of values that causes the boy to bring about his own dilemma. Until he meets Lucy, he is able to keep his middle-class values separate from those of the track. He has had to live with the values of two conflicting ways of life, for his lower middle-class family, consisting of his mother and his sister, is poor but it also has genteel notions of propriety and respectability which clash with his affinity for the track. The family is fatherless, and the boy has to work; but he is nineteen, so the odd jobs go to others smaller and younger than he. He, therefore, is both driven and drawn to work at the track; and the tension between the demands of his middle-class background and the gratifications of the track comprises the conflict within him that undermines his self-confidence. His attitudes thus vacillate between middle-class respectability and the freedom of the tracks and between his need for self-esteem and his desire for love, which he cannot reconcile in his brief, idyllic romance with Lucy.

He is not bright enough to see the incompatibility of his values. He despises people who "put on airs," yet he has always, he says, believed in putting up "a good front." The free and sentient life of the groom provides him with "a lot of valuable things for any man to know." But he is unable to specify what those things are; and, despite his "experience" at the tracks with race-fixing, drinking, brawling and lying, he is basically an innocent who responds with the uncorrupted sensitivity of youth to the immediate life of the senses: "Gee whiz, Gosh amighty, the nice hickorynut and beechnut and oaks and other kinds of trees along the roads, all brown and red, and the good smells, and Burt [the Negro trainer] singing a song that was called Deep River, and the country girls at the windows of the houses and everything."

Yet he is not entirely satisfied with the mindless life of the primitive. His assertion that "You can stick your colleges up your nose for all of me" betrays his insecurity. Furthermore, the lack of conviction in his insistence upon the superiority of life as a swipe over that of the respectable people in the grandstands is readily apparent in his desire to impress Lucy Wessen, her brother, and her brother's girl friend with his pretended background of wealth and position.

The chief weakness of this story is that the boy's naïveté deteriorates into stupidity. His inability to recognize the broad, palpable inconsistencies in his values makes him an object of contempt as well as pity, and his lack of insight into what should be obvious to a nineteen-year-old deprives the story of the ironic subtlety of "I Want to Know Why." In the latter story the boy's bafflement is made understandable by dramatic demonstration of his naïve belief that his adolescent ideal and the facts of life outside the confraternity of life at the track could be kept separated. In "I'm a Fool" the swipe's frustrated romance emanates from his stolid inability to discriminate among his allegiances. We cannot help feeling that he is indeed a fool. At times his ignorance comes close to incredibility and Anderson's mastery of rustic Midwestern dialect—which is equal in "I Want to Know Why" to the best of Twain—descends into obviousness and loses touch with its purpose. Intended to convey the boy's naïveté, it confirms his ignorance and serves as a substitute for the brilliantly enacted clash in "I Want to Know Why" between what the groom says and what he understands. When he advises Wilbur Wessen about betting on "About Ben Ahem," for instance, the boy says: "Don't bet a cent on this first heat because he'll go like an oxen hitched to a plow, but when the first heat is over go right down and lay on your pile." He knows the races are fixed, but he betrays a complete inability to make moral discriminations.

Yet, "I'm a Fool" must not be read too gravely, for it is essentially a humorous story, resembling more than anything else Ring Lardner's hyperbolic sketches of ignoramuses who trap themselves by their hilarious persistence in evading the truth. The dialogue of "I'm a Fool" is in fact comic in its exaggeration: the initial sentence sets the tone: "It was a hard jolt for me, one of the most bitterest I ever had to face." That there are, however, added dimensions of seriousness and pathos in Anderson's portrayal of the boy raises the story above Lardner's frequently thin satires.

The finest of the horses-and-men tales is "The Man Who Became a Woman," which exceeds "I Want to Know Why" in psychological depth and in symbolic richness. In this story the narrator is a man, now well past his adolescence, who is successfully married; and he tells his story not as a naïve, confused boy but as an adult recalling a youthful experience with a sense of shame and degradation and under a compulsion to cleanse himself through confession.

The story consists of two parts: the first is a long-view narrative of events leading up to the main episode, which comprises the second part and is presented "scenically." In the chief episode, Herman Dudley, the narrator, agrees one evening to stay at the stables to look after the horses while the other swipes go into town. He becomes restless and wanders off to a saloon, where a group of miners are drinking and playing cards. While sitting at the bar, he glances into the mirror at his own face and it appears to be the face of a girl. As he is recovering from the shock of what he thinks he sees, a very large man enters with his small son, and the miners begin to make remarks about the man behind his back, saying he is "cracked." When a gaudily dressed dandy among them grows bold and jeers openly at him, the man shoves his son into the arms of Herman Dudley, orders him to hold the child, and calmly but brutally beats his heckler.

Still shaken by what he has seen in the mirror and sickened by the coarseness and brutality of the men in the saloon, Dudley leaves the saloon and returns in the rain to the stables, where he takes off his wet clothes and crawls into the hayloft. Two drunken Negro swipes find him and, thinking him a girl, attempt to attack him. Thoroughly terrified, he escapes, but in his flight he stumbles into a field near a slaughter house and falls upon the skeleton of a horse and becomes enmeshed in its rib cage. The steadily mounting terror of the evening reaches its peak at this point, and, as he struggles to extricate himself, he screams. The scream releases him, calms him, and rids him finally of "that silly nonsense about being a girl." Freeing himself, he finds a haystack into which he crawls and which he shares with a flock of sheep. In the morning, he returns naked to the stables and is greeted by the laughter of the other grooms, except for his friend Burt. Finding some clothes, the boy leaves racing and the tracks for good.

The remarkable Gothic, nightmarish quality—similar to that of Faulkner's *Sanctuary*, later—of the second part of this tale is achieved by Anderson's gradual intensification of symbols of action and atmosphere which culminate in the death of the boy's cherished but doomed innocence in the rib casement of the horse's skeleton. Like the swipe in "I Want to Know Why," Dudley resists entry into adult male sexuality, clinging to his childhood world of untarnished emotional attachments, a fact established in the first part of the story where his association with the writer Tom Means is shown to be based upon their shared love for thoroughbred horses, their joy in the track fraternity, and the boy's admiration for Means's articulate idealization of horses, those untainted aristocrats of nature. With Means present, he is able to expunge the impurities from horse racing and to constrain his emerging sexual longings; for Means gives expression to those noble sentiments the boy feels about thoroughbreds and raises racing to the level of art (Means wants to write "the way a well-bred horse runs or trots or paces"). In "loving" Means, Dudley can hold on to his comfortable pre-adolescent hero worship both of Means himself and of the great Pop Geers.

When Means leaves, however, Dudley is forced to face the more complex facts of the tracks and of his own sexual maturity. Without Means, the imaginative quality that had given meaning to racing and thoroughbreds is lost, and the boy is thrust into the brutal realities of life: the trickery of the horse owners, the lust of the grooms and their "fly" girls, and his own physical needs which now turn his dreams to nightmares after which he feels like "old Harry." His resistance to the world of physical fact is a rejection of its ugliness, and it begins when he decides to stay alone at the stables. Shortly, however, he finds it impossible to remain alone; his thoughts of an ideal, undefiled woman, "slender and like a flower with something in her like a race horse too," drive him away from the stables in search of company. Destruction of his impossible ideal begins when he enters the bar, and it ends with his fall into the rib casement, which symbolizes the death of his youth in the grim, skeletal embodiment of his ideal of pure beauty.

Psychologically, he cannot remain in that youthful world and become a man; his resistance to it has already generated a confusion of his sexual longings. But the alternative is acceptance of a sordid outer world utterly lacking in beauty, so his choice is one between nightmares. And Anderson's most masterful achievement in the story is his portrayal of the boy's inner struggle—the irresistible assertion of the dark blood—in concrete dramatic and symbolic terms.

The nightmarish atmosphere of the story both weighs upon the boy's sensibility and mirrors his inner conflict. As Dudley's initial agitation grows to terror, the intensity of his actions increases with the deepening horror of the wasteland images. Matching his own physical impotence and moral confusion are the spiritual impotence and fragmentation of society, as symbolized by the countryside consisting of "stones sticking out of the ground and trees mostly of the stubby, stunted kind"; by the mining town where the long rows of coke ovens at night look "like the teeth of some big man-eating giant lying and waiting . . ."; and by the saloon, whose diabolic atmosphere reflects the brutality of the spiritually emasculated miners. The ugly facts of the outer world combine with the demands of a repressed—or at least a resisted—subconscious to force him to abandon his childhood world of ideal innocence and become a man. In Freudian terms, the "big wave" that hits him releases his male sex drives; and his scream frees him from his verbal and physical paralysis. Entering the haystack naked with the sheep, he is in a figurative sense born again into a new innocence of manhood. When he leaves the track for good, he leaves behind both an ideal impossible to maintain and a sordid reality impossible to ignore. He assumes his role in the adult world where pure non-physical innocence does not exist, where innocence compels a discriminating selection from among complex alternatives.

With the stories in *The Triumph of the Egg* and in *Horses and Men* Anderson reached the height of his genius. Only on rare occasions afterward did he rise to the quality of the better tales in these two volumes. But it was a peculiarity in him that he did not understand the real nature or limitations of his talent and so expended much of his energy upon the romance-novel and upon his special brand of prose-poems which he termed "chants," when it was already apparent by 1920 that he had done and was doing his best work in the rather confined genre of the tale. Yet he was uneasy about the limitations of his range, and the generally favorable response of men like Brooks, Mencken, and Sinclair Lewis to *Poor White* encouraged Anderson's belief in himself as a novelist, even though Rosenfeld and a number of other critics saw that, like *Windy* and *Marching Men*, the episodic parts of *Poor White* were superior to the whole. In the tales he achieved the indirection lacking in his longer efforts, which typically approached allegory as their heroes reached maturity, and in his "songs," which seldom rose above direct assertion of commonplace, primitivistic themes. Nevertheless, he was to persist, during the 1920's, to regard himself as a novelist and to direct his efforts toward mastery of the long narrative form. This miscalculation of the nature of his talent, plus the undeniable fact that his talent proved to be limited in scope, brought the beginning of a startlingly rapid decline in the quality of his work and in his reputation almost at the same time that they had hit their peak.

CHAPTER 6

The Artist as Prophet

ANDERSON MADE IT EVIDENT in "Seeds," that he reprehended a detached or even a temporarily involved tampering with the inner life. In that story, which is based largely upon Anderson's talks in 1916, with Burrow at Chateaugay Lake, a crippled woman from Iowa makes grotesque efforts to entice the men of her Chicago rooming house into her rooms, going so far at one point as to stand naked before her hall door. Yet she is frigid and deathly afraid of men, and shrinks from them when they come near. In discussing her actions, the narrator and his psychologist acquaintance take opposite views of the extent to which one may probe clinically into the secret recesses of the inner life for the purpose of "curing" a psychic illness. The narrator, speaking for Anderson, maintains that the professionally induced love the psychologist practices upon his patients violates love by rationalizing it. "The thing you want to do cannot be done," he tells the psychoanalyst. "Fool—do you expect love to be understood?" But in rejecting the synthetic love of the psychoanalyst, the narrator embraces another "cure" for the woman: sex. And, when he tells his friend LeRoy, who had been the woman's neighbor, that he could have helped her by becoming her lover, LeRoy replies, "It isn't so simple. By being sure of yourself you are in danger of losing all of the romance in life. You miss the point. Nothing in life can be settled so definitely."

The point of this story is that the inner life is a myriad of often conflicting impulses—of love and hate, revulsion and attraction, beauty and ugliness. And the inner life has been choked by "old thoughts and beliefs—seeds planted by dead men," by efforts to control it, or understand it. What the woman needed was "to be loved, to be long and quietly and patiently loved.... the disease she has is .... universal. We all want to be loved and the world has no plan for creating lovers." Like the psycho-analyst, LeRoy wants "more than anything else in the world to be clean," to be free of the doctrines and formulas that have destroyed the spontaneity and the force of love and that have made men and women grotesque and emotionally crippled.

In the complete spiritual exhaustion of both the scientist and the artist (LeRoy is a painter), we see Anderson's state-ment of the need for psychic rebirth; and the fact that the "disease" is universal indicates the need for a cultural rebirth. It is by no means coincidental that, at about the same time he called Burrow's attention to "Seeds," Anderson wrote to Brooks that he had "been reading *The Education of Henry Adams*" and felt "tremendously its importance as a piece of American writing."[1]

The Education of Henry Adams offered Anderson a rationale for the cultural and psychological reformation necessary to cure the "universal disease." Under the influence of Adams, Anderson found Chartres Cathedral a symbol of the power of sex as a civilizing force and a monument to the creative and unifying effects of a religion grounded in recognition of the mystery, fecundity, and beauty of the "dark blood." Adams saw the popu-lar influence of the Virgin Mary in the twelfth century as being basically sexual,[2] and in her power he saw the fructifying effects of sex upon art. The art of the Middle Ages found in the Louvre and the hundreds of cathedrals built in the name of Mary were cultural testaments to the centrality of sex in human creativity. It followed that the absence of great art and litera-ture—the symbols of a great culture—in America were the result of Puritanism. In the chapter "The Dynamo and the Virgin," Adams had lamented:

> The Woman had once been supreme; in France she still seemed potent, not merely as a sentiment, but as a force. Why was she unknown in America? For evidently America was ashamed of her, and she was ashamed of herself, otherwise they would not have strewn fig-leaves so profusely all over her. When she was

a true force, she was ignorant of fig-leaves, but the monthly-magazine-made American female had not a feature that would have been recognized by Adam. The trait was notorious, and often humorous, but any one brought up among Puritans knew that sex was sin. In any previous age, sex was strength. Neither art nor beauty was needed. Every one, even among Puritans, knew that neither Diana of the Ephesians nor any of the Oriental goddesses was worshipped for her beauty. She was goddess because of her force; she was the animated dynamo; she was reproduction — the greatest and most mysterious of all energies; all she needed was to be fecund.

Adams provided Anderson with a symbol for his belief (previously derived from Brooks, Rosenfeld, and Frank) that Puritanism and industrialism were historically connected, and also for his conviction that sexual repression meant death to art and beauty. Adams held that "sex was strength" for any age previous to the twentieth century. "The Venus of Epicurean philosophy survived in the Virgin of the Schools," but "all this was to American thought as though it had never existed. The true American knew something of the facts, but nothing of the feelings; he read the letter, but he never felt the law. Before this historic chasm, a mind like that of Adams felt itself helpless; he turned from the Virgin to the dynamo as though he were a Branly coherer. On one side, at the Louvre and at Chartres, as he knew by the record of work actually done and still before his eyes, was the highest energy ever known to men, the creator of four-fifths of his noblest art, exercising vastly more attraction over the human mind than all the steam engines and dynamos ever dreamed of; and yet this energy was unknown to the American mind. An American Virgin would never dare command; an American Venus would never dare exist."

This passage, one Anderson felt important enough to quote in *A Story Teller's Story*, is implicit in the themes of *Many Marriages* and of *Dark Laughter*. In *Many Marriages*, John Webster transforms his Puritanistically virgin daughter into a virgin cleansed of the notion, as Adams puts it, "that sex was sin"; she is ready to accept the "gift of life" (which, as in *Poor White*, is symbolized by some multi-colored stones he gives her). In *Dark Laughter* the hero slowly achieves understanding and acceptance of "the blood" as the central creative force in life. It was Adams, therefore, rather than D. H. Lawrence, who had the greatest influence upon Anderson's attitudes from 1920 to 1925. Despite Irving Howe's very persuasive argument that Anderson moved into "the Lawrencian orbit," Lawrence was for Anderson no more than a greatly admired fellow novelist who shared his general views on the importance of sex. Anderson found a kinship with Lawrence in their shared repugnance for bloodless spirituality and intellectualism; but Anderson, like Adams, was fighting primarily the repressiveness of American Puritanism and machine worship (Webster is a washing-machine manufacturer) rather than the more intellectually formidable European *haute monde* who populated Lawrence's works. It would no doubt have been well had Anderson taken lessons from Lawrence; for, if he had studied *The Rainbow* and *Women in Love* with care, he might have learned that symbols and symbolic acts alone are not enough to carry a thesis which purports to comprehend all the complex facets of life.

I Many Marriages

Many Marriages is shaped, from beginning to end, by the proposition that by lifting the lid of moral repression from the inner life one may release the manifold impulses of the subconscious and enjoy a multitude of beautiful relationships and "many marriages." A small-town businessman nearing forty, John Webster suddenly falls in love with his secretary and decides to leave his family and his business and to live with her in another city. Though there has been no love in his family since his marriage, he feels obliged to explain his decision to his daughter Jane and to try to save her from the kind of sterile, purposeless life he has renounced. Resolving to "bring life" to her by teaching her of "this other, this inner" life of love and of the finer feelings which demand sensual expression, he brings both Jane and his wife to his bedroom, and, standing naked before them, delivers a night-long lecture that is interlarded with soul-searching interior monologues containing reminiscences about his marriage and explanations for its failure, reflections about the social and historical causes behind the plight of modern men, and assertions about the necessity of freeing the sexual impulses in order to liberate the inner life. He observes: "If one kept the lid off the well of thinking within oneself, let the well empty itself, let the mind consciously think any thoughts that came to it, accepted all thinking, all imaginings, as one accepted the flesh of people, animals, birds, trees, plants, one might live a hundred or a thousand lives in one life." At the end of the long night, Webster leaves; his wife poisons herself; and Jane, now awakened like Mary Cochran in "The Door of the Trap," is ostensibly free to receive all the impulses of life.

In the central episode of the story, Webster places a picture of the Virgin Mary on his bedroom dresser, flanks the picture with two candlesticks bearing figures of Christ on the cross, and paces naked before the picture. After several nights of this ritual exercise, he manages at last to draw Jane and his wife to the room, where they observe the ceremony in shocked bewilderment. As symbols, the Virgin and the two icons bring into association Webster's rite and the idea of the sanctity of sex, and his nakedness signifies his own purification and rebirth through acceptance of the senses. The picture has two rhetorical functions. First, it supports Webster's effort to persuade his daughter that the Puritan morality by which she was brought up is a denial of life; for, as he explains to her that his startling act was necessary to properly arrest and hold her attention, he declares: "I have a desire to in some way make the flesh a sacred thing to you." Second, the Virgin symbol suggests the notion of sex as a creative, unifying force. Anderson's thesis is that sex is the agency by which all the senses come to life and through which the inner creative life of the imagination is set free; the picture of the Virgin represents—to him as it did to Adams—the symbolic synthesis of physical and spiritual love that unites rather than separates people and ultimately expresses itself in the beauty of art.

The chief weakness of *Many Marriages* is that the symbols— of which the picture of the Virgin is one of the most important—

are made to carry a greater rhetorical burden than they can bear, being used in lieu of action to convey the themes. Anderson's thesis is not imaginatively realized through either symbols or action, and the novel lapses therefore into mere rhetoric. Limited largely to Webster's reflections about life, which begin in puzzled wonderment and end in complacent, almost arrogant self-assurance, the narrative is hopelessly burdened by direct assertion, which in the absence of action almost undermines the thesis; for Webster confirms his own stupidity and egotism in his protracted soul-searching, his certainty that what he smugly calls his insanity is really the only sanity, his cruel denunciation and degradation of his wife in the presence of his daughter, and his absurdly clinical erotic tampering with his daughter. The assertions about his daughter in the following passage, for instance, have no scenic support and betray Webster's vanity and self-satisfaction in his new-found freedom: "His daughter was standing in the doorway leading to her own room, looking at him, and there was a kind of intense half-insane mood in her as all evening there had been in him. He had infected her with something out of himself. After all there had been what he had wanted, a real marriage. After this evening the younger woman could never be what she might have been, had this evening not happened. Now he knew what he wanted for her."

Many Marriages is a thoroughly irresponsible work, both artistically and intellectually; but we need not question Anderson's integrity of purpose. The irresponsibility consists in his failure to condense his material, to tighten the structure of the book, and to examine the nature and consequences of his themes and the assumptions behind them. Above all, it is irresponsible because his mouthpiece, Webster, wins his argument too easily; he has no articulate antagonist to challenge his assumptions. In the absence of any discernible dialectic or narrative conflict, Webster's supposedly sophisticated ideas about life and sex become the maunderings of a terribly ignorant man, and his symbolic act of psychic and physical rebirth is reduced to absurdity.

II Dark Laughter

Dark Laughter, which reveals Anderson's admiration for the stream-of-consciousness techniques of James Joyce, is a somewhat more successful effort at a "sophisticated" treatment of the need for "blood consciousness" than is *Many Marriages.* But *Dark Laughter* is thoroughly artificial in style and characterization and only slightly better than the earlier book in dramatic enactment of its thesis. Like his Adamic predecessors, the hero breaks with convention and tries to find meaning in his own life by "entering into" the lives of others. A journalist and an aspiring writer, he abandons his newspaper job in Chicago and his wife. He is a writer and intellectual whose anti-conventionalist intellectualism is in itself conventional. He goes back to the small town of his youth, an Ohio River town in Indiana called Old Harbor, where he assumes the name Bruce Dudley and takes a job in a wheel factory owned by Fred Grey. Anderson's diagnosis of the social illness that drives Dudley to Old Harbor, and his use of primitivistic imagery are similar to those in his four earlier romances: "He [Dudley] had a vague notion that he, in common with almost all American men, had got out of touch with things—stones lying in fields, the fields themselves, houses, trees, rivers, factory walls, tools, women's bodies, sidewalks, men in overalls, men and women in automobiles."

At the factory he becomes friendly with Sponge Martin, a craftsman and a primitive who symbolizes instinctive self-fulfillment in the creativeness of his trade and in his frank, uninhibited response to the promptings of the flesh, particularly his sexual relations with his wife. Martin is contrasted with Fred Grey, a typically impotent Andersonian businessman whose emotional poverty is reflected in sexual inadequacy. Dudley and Grey's wife Aline, whom he sees waiting for Grey outside the factory gate, are instantly attracted to one another; and, when after a period of time he becomes her gardener and lover, she leaves Grey and goes away with Dudley.

The similarity between Anderson's Fred and Aline Grey and Dudley and D. H. Lawrence's Lord and Lady Chatterley and Mellors (Lawrence's work came later) is palpable enough, as is the theme that sex is at once the culmination of physical and spiritual love and the fountainhead of human self-fulfillment. The Joycean influence is apparent in the awkward stream-of-conscious style carrying the rambling thought of Dudley who, somewhat like Bloom and Dedalus in *Ulysses,* is searching for the source of his being. But *Dark Laughter* can hardly be compared qualitatively with either *Lady Chatterley's Lover* or with *Ulysses,* for, like *Many Marriages,* it consists largely of the reflections of the principal characters, Bruce Dudley and Aline Grey, about the complexity of life and the mess people make of it. Moreover, their wandering recollections and self-analyses impede rather than advance or generate action. Dudley is a dreamer and cannot, like his friend Sponge Martin, act upon his impulses. It is Aline who initiates their affair, secures him as her gardener, and takes the final steps to bring about their union. This weakness in the character of Dudley comprises the chief weakness of the book; for, lacking indirect expression through action, his reflections are obvious and affected and in fact represent an escape from rather than a movement toward the desired response to the natural impulses.

The Torrents of Spring, which was prompted by *Dark Laughter* and aimed most specifically at it, points among other things to the irrelevance of themes to action in the repeated scenes Hemingway draws involving incredibly literary and intellectual waitresses who cite Henry James and read the *Manchester Guardian* for no reason explainable in the narrative. *Torrents* also pillories those stylistic and structural affectations that accompany the paucity of action: absurd rhetorical questions about trivial matters, intended to invest those matters with "mystery"; frequent sentence fragments designed to render the fragmentary nature of the mind in operation but too often effecting a disingenuous tone; and the disjunctive structure, ostensibly conceived to further delineate the movement of a mind groping and searching back and forth in time but impressing the reader as an ostentatious contempt for form.

Dark Laughter is an unsuccessful effort to combine a highly sophisticated Joycean stream-of-consciousness style and structure with the simple rhythms of New Orleans jazz and to bring two sophisticated people, Bruce Dudley and Aline Grey, to simple acceptance of the senses—as symbolized by the "dark laughter" of the Negroes who move in the background throughout the story. Once more, Anderson's solution to the problems of the individual in relation to society and to himself is oversimplified. We are left to wonder where Bruce and Aline go from Mudcat Landing and what they do in the face of the same problems that existed before they fell in love. Having shown the need to repudiate conventional values, Anderson is obligated to prove in authentic narrative terms that the alternatives his characters embrace are workable, as he indicates they are. He suggests that the union of Bruce and Aline brings an end to their problems, but the feeling remains that it merely represents a new beginning and that, while they may have achieved the uncomplicated response to the senses of Sponge Martin and the Negroes, they will hardly be able, in light of their conditioning by the refinements of cultivated society, to adopt the simple primitivism Martin and the Negroes symbolize.

More than anything else, *Many Marriages* and *Dark Laughter* demonstrate that a simple blood consciousness and freedom from sexual inhibitions can hardly solve the problems of a complex modern life for sophisticated, complicated people. And, when Anderson purports to portray the workability of such simplistic solutions, his "sophisticated" characters turn out after all to be simple-minded and confused.

III   D. H. Lawrence and Freud

In reference to Lawrence's *Studies in Classic American Literature*, Anderson commented to Alfred Steiglitz that "when [Lawrence] tells a story, he is fine; when he lays down his principles, I think him a pretentious fool. He dreams of being the great, dark animal. It is, after all, a neurotic wish."[3] With more temperate language, Anderson could just as well have said the same thing about himself. His cultural and psychological primitivism was based upon an even less critical anti-intellectualism and irrationalism than was Lawrence's. If Lawrence's rejection of reason as a guide to human conduct left him little to go by except the instincts—which he sanctified ("my religion is the blood")—he nevertheless had considerable first-hand acquaintance with ideas which enabled him to make distinctions necessary to a fairly tenable primitivistic position.

For one thing, Lawrence never regarded reversion to a less civilized state, which Anderson suggests in the simple sensuality of the Negroes, as an answer to contemporary cultural failure; and so Lawrence never fell into the impracticable cultural primitivism of *Dark Laughter*. Moreover, Lawrence read Freud, which Anderson claimed he never did; and he was able to come to grips with the complexities of sex as Anderson never could. As Frederick Hoffman has well demonstrated,[4] Lawrence was fully aware of the intricacies of the sex instinct as defined by Freud and was able to deal brilliantly—if not always defensibly—with Freudian descriptions of subtle relationships between the conscious and the unconscious. He was capable, after careful study of Freud, of accepting some of Freud's principles and rejecting others. With considerable self-assurance, he could affirm the vitalism of the unconscious and the centrality of sex as a life-generating force and reject Freud's conception of the ego as a desirable intellectual, moral and social deterrent to the excesses of the id, or unconscious, which Lawrence maintained was corrupted rather than moderated by the ego.

Anderson first learned his Freud on what Hoffman has called the summary or survey level, from articulate laymen, like Dell, who read Freud in translation and passed their general understanding on to others.[5] Anderson's introduction to the new psychology came shortly after his arrival in Chicago in 1913. At Chateaugay Lake in 1916—when he was writing the *Winesburg* tales—he met Burrow and had the discussions with him that culminated in "Seeds." While Burrow later told Hoffman that Anderson "very definitely" did not read Freud nor "draw any material from what he knew of Freud through others,"[6] he subsequently corrected himself and conceded that "it would now appear that Anderson was not influenced by my talks with him on psychoanalysis." His own chief interest, Burrow went on, was in what seemed to him "the social implications of the neurosis and it was this aspect of our talk that took a strong hold with Anderson."[7] Burrow emphasized once more what he had told Hoffman: "that Sherwood Anderson was an original psychologist in his own right and, if he profited by any insights of mine, I also profited in no small measure by the exceptional insight of his literary genius."[8]

The truth of Burrow's comment in his letter to Hoffman that "Anderson was a man of amazing intuitive flashes but. . . . like Freud, the chief source of his material was his own uncanny insight" is readily apparent when we once more regard *Many Marriages* and *Dark Laughter* in the light of "Seeds." In contrast to the romances—in which he develops a thesis about the "social implications" of neurosis—his theme in "Seeds" comes through in brief, penetrating insights into the needs of all men through portrayals of the psychoanalyst, the artist, and the woman from Iowa. In other words, he analyzes his characters in the story without setting forth in narrative terms his thesis that the ills of the world could be cured by a greater consciousness of the "dark blood." Anderson repeatedly rejected Freudian formulas, for he resisted what he regarded as the oversimplification of the human mind and heart. He resented the tendency of the popular psychoanalysis he was acquainted with to generate self-consciousness and inhibitions by labeling an individual's expressions and gestures with pat phrases. His steadfast refusal to accept such systematization and oversimplification is what Burrow found most engaging and brilliant in him, and his own artist's reliance on his imaginative projection into the inner lives of others and absorption of those lives finds its best expression in such great tales as "Seeds." Where Anderson develops a thesis, as he does in *Many Marriages* and *Dark Laughter,* he falls into the same oversimplification the psychoanalyst and narrator do in "Seeds"; and he becomes even more liable than Lawrence to the charge that he "dreams of being the great, dark animal," which is, "after all, a neurotic wish."

The romance was clearly not Anderson's form. When he wanted to deal with "ideas," he did his best work in the imaginative autobiography or "confession," a form admirably suited to his best narrative style of intimate, subjective commentary. Such a work is *A Story Teller's Story.*

IV   A Story Teller's Story

In *The Anatomy of Criticism,* Northrop Frye terms one of his hybrid forms the romance-confession, which he defines as the fictionalized "autobiography of a romantic temperament." "Nearly always some theoretical and intellectual interest in religion, politics, or art plays a leading role in the confession," Frye writes. "It is his success in integrating his mind on such subjects that makes the author of a confession feel that his life is worth writing about."[9] He adds that the familiar essay bears the same formal relation to the confession that the tale has to the romance and that the short story has to the novel. *A Story Teller's Story* may best be defined as a romance-confession made up of familiar essays that are held together—like the tales in *Winesburg*—by a common theme and by a mythical rather than a chronological structural sequence. Because it remains close to Anderson's own experience, it is vastly superior both artistically and rhetorically to *Many Marriages* and to *Dark Laughter.*

In spite of the sometimes annoying tone of calculated naïveté interspersed with lapses into pretentious cultural sophistication; notwithstanding the occasionally digressive "Notes" that too often mar the internal coherence; and despite the superfluous epilogue about a corrupted American writer, *A Story Teller's Story* contains some of Anderson's finest writing. While it hardly deserves to be classed with *Walden* or with *Leaves of Grass,* it does share two qualities with those masterpieces. First, it has an intangible but pervasive quality which suggests the presence of an authentic person and of a vital, sensitive inner life moving through successive stages of struggle with the world of fact but left finally to nourish itself with rare "moments" of beauty of life and art. As in *Walden* and in *Leaves of Grass,* we are aware at all times of an immediate and sustained link with a personality who dominates his material but is inseparable from it and whose essential life has been fashioned out of the great struggle of his imagination to achieve integrity. Second, it shares with these two books a structural cohesion and movement which have unfortunately gone unappreciated by most critics but which make the book a significant expression of the "American myth." Admittedly—almost defiantly—an imaginative biography, it deliberately scorns the primacy of the world of fact and compels an imaginative, mythical interpretation.

Because Anderson transforms the essence of both his imaginative and factual life into a fable that brings together the chief skeins of his own experience and the myth of the American Adam, he succeeds in doing what he could not do in any of his books except *Poor White*: he finds an intellectually defensible, if not practicable, attitude or thesis, based not on a course of social action or simple blood consciousness but on a state of mind. As Frederic I. Carpenter has ably shown, the American Adam myth has involved an imagined redemption as well as a fall.[10] The American Adam has helped destroy his great primitive paradise, but he has become wiser; and, in his new wisdom, he perceives his kinship with that paradise and pursues a course of wise innocence, glimpsing thereby a "paradise to be regained." In all his romances Anderson's heroes follow this course; but in *Windy, Marching Men, Many Marriages,* and *Dark Laughter* we are given to believe that in family life, in psychological collectivism, or in blood consciousness, a paradise of renewed innocence may be realized. *A Story Teller's Story* has a more defensible thesis than any of these novels because Anderson ends the book with the ambiguities and dilemmas implicit throughout the narrative.

The point of view is that of the self-confident, successful author who nostalgically recalls his development as a writer, recollects the factual and fanciful life of his youth, points to the facts of life which misdirected his imaginative endowment and sent him into the "ugly" world of fact, relates the struggle between his imaginative nature and the demands of a business society that led to his break from business, and tells of his quest for critical guidance and for esthetic and moral integrity in America. In typical Anderson fashion, the narrative sequence moves back and forth in time; but, overall, the book has a discernible development which is psychological and chronological as well as mythical.

Moving back and forth in a kind of psychological continuum,

the narrative progresses by means of an accretion of concrete incidents that cluster about the four successively higher stages of the artist's psychic development: (1) his small-town youth, the time of fancy, sentience, and innocence; (2) his young manhood in Chicago, the awakening to "a consciousness of something wrong" and a reaching out for a meaningful connection with life; (3) his plunge into the world of fact, of business and the success ethic, and the rebellion of the inner life and purification ("a sweet clean feeling") and rebirth in the act of becoming a writer; (4) the construction of a new life, the "pilgrimage" of the artist, as the prototype of the "whole man," in search of psychic and sentient integrity and simplicity.

Each stage of development is constructed loosely about a symbolic character or group who have contributed to his imaginative heritage or growth. In Book I we see the stage of youthful fancy and innocence. The natural demand of the fancy is for a role, an identity, a heroic conception of self, and for union with others. The symbolic figure in this section is his father, Irwin Anderson. In a series of parallels between himself as a boy and his father, Anderson discloses the glories and the dangers of the romantic fancy and concurrently frames his esthetic theories in narrative terms. The father's yarn-spinning, directed in one episode toward the farm girl Tillie, is a kind of love-making which takes both the storyteller and the listener out of themselves and unites them in an almost mystical embrace. "In the world of fancy . . . no man is ugly. Man is ugly in fact only." The demands of the fancy are for love and beauty, and in it "all morality . . . becomes a purely esthetic matter. What is beautiful must bring esthetic joy; what is ugly must bring esthetic sadness and suffering."

In the father's tale of his own heroism and tragedy during the Civil War, he illustrates the dangers inherent to the fancy. Where it has nothing in the real world upon which to fix itself, it becomes an instrument of escape; and, driven in upon itself, it causes grotesqueness, egocentricity, and disorder. The adult imagination comes into being when the youthful, romantic fancy is brought to bear upon the recalcitrant world of fact, when

the youthful luxury of pure and innocent dreams gives way to
a conscious effort to shape the world of fact and sense to its
ideal of beauty. In his father's childish innocence, Anderson
sees a symbol of America in its immaturity: a people still unable
to bring the needs of the fancy for love and beauty to bear
upon its material life.

Book II begins with his first experience in Chicago and is
built upon a series of contrasts depicting the painful process
of facing the facts of life. Plunged into the grim, factual world
of Chicago, the narrator's mind moves nostalgically back in
time to Clyde and to Judge Turner, who first awakened his
imagination to the possibility of beauty in the life of actuality
in telling him of Chartres Cathedral. At this stage of the artist's
pilgrimage, the fancy shrinks away from "a world where only
men of action seemed to thrive" and which was symbolized by
the Ford.

In this section Anderson relates his growing sickness as his
revulsion from industrial squalor and from the tired, dirty,
defeated people broadened the chasm between his inner and
outer life. "I lay on my back," he writes of his early days in
Chicago, "trying to get up courage to face facts." The unsatis-
fied demands of the fancy drove him to writing, but "I was
always trying to create in a world of my fancy and that was
always being knocked galley-west by the facts of my life." He
was drawn reluctantly into the difficult world of fact by Alonzo
Berners, a young man crippled and beaten by life who "simply
loved the people about him and the places in which they lived
and . . . that [had] become a force in itself affecting the very
air people breathed."

This Berners episode sets the stage for Book III, in which
Anderson explains his entry into business as a kind of "fortunate
fall" in which his imaginative life fixed itself upon the "unstated
but dimly understood American dream" of making himself "a
successful man in the business world." The central "character"
in this book is the nameless, faceless mass of Americans who
are grotesquely absorbed in their own affairs. Like the original
Adam of the Old Testament, he discovers evil; and his moral
life begins when psychological revulsion initiates an awareness

that the great evil in life is egoism and that Puritanism, industrialism, and the success ethic are not only social manifestations but also causes of self-love. Supporting this moral discovery is consciousness of the historical myth of the garden and awareness of the failure of America to live up to its promise: "This vast land was to be a refuge for all the outlawed brave foolish folk of the world." There was to be a new beginning, a new chance for man: "The declaration of the rights of man was to have a new hearing in a new place." But "something went wrong."

> They built the cathedral of Chartres to the glory of God and we really intended building here a land to the glory of Man, and thought we were doing it too. That was our intention and the affair only blew up in the process, or got perverted, because Man, even the brave and the free Man, is somewhat a less worthy object of glorification than God. This we might have found out long ago but that we did not know each other. We came from too many different places to know each other well, had been promised too much, wanted too much. We were afraid to know each other.

Constructed around too climactic moments of discovery, Book III relates (1) Anderson's sudden realization that his life as a businessman was unclean, his "overwhelming feeling of uncleanliness," his abandonment of business—partly as a response to psychological necessity—and (2) his entry into a new world purified of egoism and demanding a new morality. Book IV presents the building of that new moral world. The chief symbols, the Virgin and the Dynamo, represent the culmination of his now-conscious quest for a symbol of the good life. This chapter traces his quest in the East among the intellectuals, whose absorption with ideas destroyed any sentient and emotional contact with life and art; the chapter ends with the climactic, epiphanous moment at Chartres, when with Rosenfeld he sat entranced before the great Cathedral and found at last the symbol of imaginative fulfillment in love and art, the symbol of a whole people welded together for the creation of beauty. "It was one of the best moments of my own life. . . . In the presence of the beautiful old church one was only more aware, all art could do no more than that—make people, like my friend and myself, more aware . . ." of the "tragic-comic sweet way" of life. Anderson had at last found his symbol of human perfection. It remained now to turn from the past to the future—with the qualities embodied by the Cathedral as the goal—to America with a new understanding of the nature and possibilities of art.

Students of American literature would do well to look more closely and favorably at *A Story Teller's Story*, particularly as a definition of the condition of the artist in America. As Anderson portrays it, that condition is scarcely encouraging, and yet a note of hope for the future of art in America persists as a kind of undertone which surges up during the moment at Chartres when Anderson decides that, for better or worse, "The future of the western world lay with America." Like its immediate predecessor, *The Education of Henry Adams, A Story Teller's Story* does not violate the ambiguities and self-contradictions its author encounters in his quest for an understanding of his world; rather, it maintains them, and as Anderson accepts without attempting to alter the conditions of American life— neither despairing nor affirming a cheap, accommodating optimism—we feel some of the tragedy that goes with being an artist in America.

CHAPTER 7

Artist as Radical: the
Social Romance

DESPITE THE DISMAL and depressing failure of *Many Marriages* and of *Dark Laughter,* Anderson's fiction during 1923-25 was by no means uniformly bad. If he had not mastered the romance as an art form, and if those two books proved that he was artistically and intellectually unequipped to render a thesis in credible narrative terms, he was still master of the tale. He could yet tell a tender but penetrating, haunting story of unpretentious, grotesque people whose grotesqueness has within it a precious essence that confirms their humanity and affirms their worth. By 1925, the quarry from which he drew his materials for those tales was almost exhausted; and, in view of the increasing sophistication of the 1920's, it is understandable enough that he felt, as he wrote to his friend Ferdinand Schevill, he couldn't "go on writing in an old mood— the naïve people of a small town."[1] Nevertheless, it was in that mood that he did his best writing, and out of the many failures of these years two tales shine forth with all the brilliance of his finest, earlier achievements.

In addition to being a touching—if not factually precise—portrayal of the young William Faulkner, "A Meeting South" is a warm, rich story of a satisfying, idyllic evening in New Orleans. Almost devoid of plot, it relates the meeting of a young Southerner who is in constant pain from a war wound and must drink to get relief, and a sixty-five year old ex-Midwestern woman, Aunt Sally, who has owned a New Orleans gambling house for thirty years and is now "retired." Because of the man's intense suffering and his quiet, unpretentious courage and the woman's long experience with gamblers, prostitutes, and clandestine lovers, these characters reveal depths and shades of sensibility that make the narrator profoundly happy. The young man is at once a romantic, a poet who wants to write like Shelley, and a delicately wrought but stoically proud Southern aristocrat. Aunt Sally is a woman with a most questionable past, judged by the conventional standards Anderson never tired of flaunting, but she is also an aristocrat herself in her sensitivity and understanding.

All the elements of the full, abundant life of the senses and affections are present in the story to please the narrator: sounds of people singing; the fragrance of the lantana and a China-berry tree; the luxuriant beauty of the Rose of Montana blooming "madly" against a patio wall; the frank, free, unashamed lustiness of a group of sailors and of Aunt Sally; the romance of a city steeped in traditions, enriched by a code of manners, and enlivened by frankly sensual people—and still unpolluted by Northern industrialism and convention; the presence of the Negroes with their uninhibited acceptance of the senses; and the good companionship of a young man absorbed in poetry and experienced in suffering that has killed all traces of egotism. In the background moves the mysterious, treacherous, beneficent mother-symbol of life, the Mississippi River. The story is unique in the absence of grotesqueness. David's agonized suffering and Aunt Sally's conventionally shady past signify depth and breadth of experience rather than the privation of the typical Andersonian grotesques. Yet, like the tales of the grotesques, "A Meeting South" synthesizes the feelings of the narrator, and Anderson transforms a simple incident into an intricate texture of complex emotions. The chief difference between this tale and the stories of the grotesques is that the narrator experiences a glowing sense of emotional, imaginative, and sensuous fulfillment.

By contrast, "Death in the Woods"—which appeared in its earliest form in *Tar: A Midwest Childhood* and is by far the best selection in that book—portrays human privation so complete that it passes into the realm of natural beauty. Rendering of such a difficult theme requires a language that presses beyond the reach of prose into poetry, and the care Anderson gave to his style is attested to by the fact that he worked over the story periodically for seven years before it was published in its final form as the title piece of *Death in the Woods*.

Like "I Want to Know Why," the story is told by a narrator, now older, who has had the incident on his mind for a number of years and can unfold its effects upon him and understand its meanings only by relating it. He gives all the facts he knows and sums up the obvious meaning of the tale; but the real meaning of the story lies in the total effect the episode has upon the teller himself. It concerns a farm woman—old at the age of forty—who spent her life feeding animals, including the "animal hunger" of her brutal and negligent husband and son. Returning home from the village one winter night with a bag of food strapped on her shoulder, she sat down to rest beneath a tree, fell into an exhausted sleep, and froze to death. When she was found a day or two later, she lay face down in the snow. Her clothes had been torn from her body and the sack of food ripped open and emptied by her four dogs, which had dragged her body into the clearing as they pulled at the bag tied to her shoulder. In the snow was a circular path made by the dogs during the night.

Anderson so intensifies the details of this magnificent tale that the most humble of human activities take on mystical significance. Two thematic strands run through the narrative: the pathos implicit in the complete privation of the woman's life and the narrator's sense of wonder at the experience of seeing her dead body in the snow. "A thing so complete" as her privation, the narrator observes, "has its own beauty," and it is the beauty that inheres in the death of this woman whose life was so totally devoid of beauty that impels him "to try to tell the simple story over again."

The picture which implants itself indelibly and brings the two thematic skeins together is that of the old woman, beautiful and young-looking in death, lying in the snow and surrounded by the oval path made by the dogs. In this scene, which Anderson presents as a kind of silent tableau, all the contrasts and paradoxes—the haunting, mysterious, mystical dramas of life and death—gather themselves in a self-contained symbolic portrait. Framed by the oval path, the dead woman's body, which in life had been old and worn out, is "white and lovely . . . like marble" under a full moon: only in death is her beauty evident; only in death do other people give her any thought— the men and boys who stare at her body in silent awe are "mystified." As a feeder of animals and men, the woman has been so thoroughly subservient, alone, and without identity and love that there is a kind of grotesque harmony and beauty in her absolute human negation, a primitive meaningfulness hidden in her complete degradation. "The whole thing, the story of the old woman's death," the narrator concludes, "was to me as I grew older like music heard from far off." For him, the scene became a part of his imaginative life; and, mystified, he unconsciously experienced the complex, paradoxical nature of beauty and took on a new consciousness of what life is worth. The strange atavistic ritual of the dogs, a reversion to a wild primitive state, emphasizes the residue of beauty and the essential mystery that lies at even the most basic levels of life.

The narrative moves from fact to mystery, ordinariness to wonderment, recollection to imaginative perception. The concreteness and simplicity of diction and the carefully balanced rhythms of the opening sentences suggest the stark simplicity of the woman's life but hint also at her mysteriousness:

> She was an old woman and lived on a farm near the town in which I lived. All country and small-town people have seen such old women, but no one knows much about them. Such an old woman comes into town driving an old worn-out horse or she comes afoot carrying a basket. She may own a few hens and have eggs to sell. She brings them in a basket and takes them to a grocer. There she trades them in. She gets some salt pork and some beans. Then she gets a pound or two of sugar and some flour.

The closing lines, with the vague "thing" and "something" and the abstract musical figures, demonstrate the sense of mystery with which the experience has left the narrator: "The whole thing, the story of the woman's death, was to me as I grew older like music heard from far off. The notes had to be picked up slowly one at a time. Something had to be understood."

Like "A Meeting South," "Death in the Woods" has an almost idyllic quality; a soft, low tone of tranquil recollection and a prose so spare and simple that, like the old woman herself, it has the music of language stripped of all except its rhythmic essence. Like the greatest of short stories, it ascends into the realm of poetry.

Despite occasional passages of writing almost as brilliant as the chapter which later became "Death in the Woods," *Tar* as a whole signifies for Anderson the exhaustion of his quarry of materials about childhood and adolescent experience. While he was able in that chapter to capture again the tone of the bewildered narrator groping to understand the complex feelings generated by a strange experience, *Tar* for the most part has a false ring, chiefly because the point of view and tone are too deliberately naïve and the innocence of its child-protagonist too soothing to disturb the equanimity of the most complacent reader. At its worst, the book descends into the kind of "cuteness" that was likely to please the subscribers of the *Woman's Home Companion* who read it in its serialized version.

Nothing indicates the personal and literary situation for Anderson in the years after 1925 more clearly than his comment to his son Robert in November, 1929: "I had a world, and it slipped away from me. The War blew up more than the bodies of men. . . . It blew ideas away—Love God Romance."[2] Both John Webster of *Many Marriages* and Bruce Dudley in *Dark Laughter* had tried to reject the present and to return to a simpler life. *Tar* was a nostalgic remembrance of the relatively uncomplicated pre-industrial small-town life of his youth, a studied effort to regain the innocence of that earlier age by affirming it. In neither of the two novels did Anderson show how his supposedly sophisticated heroes—ostensibly wise in their commitment to the "blood" and to the senses—could live in a society they had rejected but could not escape. And *Tar* signified, if nothing else, that his childhood past was dead—both as social fact and as literary source. Yet he clung to his primitivism,

and he refused to accept the facts of twentieth-century industrialism.

In Marion, Virginia, he assumed the role of country squire
and small-town editor. It soon became evident, however, that
he could not—as he left us to assume John Webster and Bruce
Dudley could—merely trade a too complicated and sophisticated
life for a very simple one, or reject entirely the twentieth century
for a mountain-village remnant of the nineteenth. In 1929, he
wrote to Robert Anderson that in *No God,* which he never
completed, he was "telling the story of a man having his roots
in the pre-War life, accepting the present day post-War life." He
had fought against sex repressions, but the times had passed
him by: "Why talk of sex repressions now? Apparently there
aren't any."[3] He had rejected Chicago and New York for the
simple life among mountain folk; and, out of his wanderings
through the hills around Marion, he accumulated the impressions of the hill-folk that became the materials for such admirable but minor sketches as "These Mountaineers," which
were collected in *Death in the Woods.* But, as his letters amply
show during this time, he was lonely; and, as the months went
by and his imaginative vitality did not return to him as he had
expected it to in that uncomplicated atmosphere, he became
increasingly depressed. After his divorce from Elizabeth early
in 1929, that depression hung like a "black dog" upon him. He
was once more near the point of breakdown.

The writing of *Beyond Desire* and a new commitment to the
cause of labor helped restore him to health once more. But in
both cases his performance was uncritical and confused. In
August, 1932, he joined Waldo Frank and a self-appointed dele-
gation of writers in a pilgrimage to Washington to protest to
President Hoover against the government's treatment of the
soldier's bonus marchers. That ill-conceived effort ended at the
desk of a Presidential secretary who refused to let them see
the President. In 1932, to Edmund Wilson's request for his
signature on a pamphlet titled "Culture and the Crisis" supporting William Z. Foster as the Communist candidate for President, Anderson responded with permission to sign his name to
that and to any similar paper.

Beyond Desire reveals both his militant concern about the workingman and his confusion as to what course should be followed to improve the worker's lot. The chief problem of the book is the same as that of *Marching Men*: Anderson's real concern is moral, and the collectivism he supports is essentially psychological rather than political and economic. The hero, Red Oliver, follows basically the same Adamic quest for innocence: psychic communion with others, as had his predecessors in Anderson's romance-novels. Like Beaut McGregor, he identifies himself with the workers in their struggle against intrenched financial and industrial power. After a long period of indecision and inaction he joins a Communist group carrying on a strike in a small North Carolina mill town; and, when the officer in command of the troops sent to break the strike threatens to shoot "like a dog" the first man to step forward, Red Oliver steps forward and is shot and killed. He achieves in his self-sacrifice a communion "beyond desire" with the oppressed workers.

To Burton Emmett in 1930, Anderson explained that what he wanted to do was to "try to humanize modern industry somewhat by making everybody more aware of the man in the factory."[4] *Beyond Desire* is proof, among other things, of the inadequacy of awareness without guidelines to political and economic implementation. Anderson characteristically rejected social theory, particularly Marxism; he stated emphatically that he was "not planning to go into the Communist Party. . . ."[5] But he had nothing other than his feeling that men should be brothers to offer in opposition to an overwhelmingly powerful capitalistic system. His total lack of intellectual direction is reflected in the main character himself and in the style and structure of the book.

Red Oliver is a compound of vague feelings which lead him into situations with which he cannot cope because his inability to sort out and to articulate his feelings paralyzes all action. All the characters, in fact, seem defeated and ineffectual; but their defeat—which Anderson attempts to prove is a social thing—is really a result of the fact that their feelings have been almost completely untouched by cerebration or by anything resembling imaginative insight. Red wants desperately the communion with women which sex offers, and he longs for that state of feeling "beyond desire" which would unite him in spirit with others. But his one sexual experience is initiated by a woman librarian who seduces him, and, each time he is given an opportunity to act effectively in identifying himself with others, he fails to perform at the crucial moment, partly because he cannot face public disapprobation and partly because he cannot accept the "cruelly logical" doctrines of the Communists. Yet we never see him try to formulate any intelligent collectivist substitute for communism; he is guided simply by his sympathy for the workers. Anderson obviously wishes us to believe that his final act is a deliberate one, and it is; but it is, nevertheless, a response to a situation created by someone else. Red's act in the end is not really, therefore, a result of deep conviction but merely a misguided and futile gesture of martyrdom.

The book is incoherent, and we need read only a few pages to see that Anderson's vision was badly confused, that he could not reconcile his belief in the necessity of collective action with his conviction that more important than collective action was spiritual communion which had nothing to do with political or economic matters. What Anderson, like Red Oliver, is interested in is fraternity, not dialectical materialism; but, considering the social inequality he portrays, it is difficult to accept the notion that spiritual union can come about without an intelligent, collective effort against political and economic inequality. Lacking an intelligible theme, the book consists of mood-fragments which have no cohesion. At times the style descends into absurdity as in the passage, "Did she care? She did care. She didn't care." At other times it is so pointlessly repetitious and so almost childishly sloppy, that it recalls Faulkner's comment that Anderson finally came to rely on style alone after he ceased to have anything to say: "The river was always yellow.... It was golden yellow. It was yellow against a blue sky. It was against trees and bushes. It was a sluggish river."

Anderson, aware of where the book's weaknesses lay, resolved to avoid them in *Kit Brandon*. To Dreiser in 1935 he wrote, "I know that you think the novel is not my field, but I may make it yet. I am trying, this time, to get a bit more outside, not quite so much surrender to pure feeling, more observation—more mind, if I have it."[6] And to Maxwell Perkins he cited the comment of a friend: "The trouble with you, Sherwood, as regards novels is that you chase moods as most men chase women." He himself added that he had almost always "tried to work out of pure feeling" under the conviction that if he "got the feeling straight and pure enough, the form . . . would follow."[7] In his last major work of fiction, *Kit Brandon*, he resolved to be "more objective, keep the whole story definitely on two or three people, the whole centering upon one. . . ."

I Kit Brandon

In *Kit Brandon*, Anderson avoided the spurious stylistic simplicity and the confused perspective of *Beyond Desire* by writing from the point of view of a sophisticated observer who, somewhat like Conrad's Marlowe, reconstructs the story as it has been told to him and as he himself was involved in it. The narrator plays the role of reflective biographer; he is the sympathetic reporter-interpreter who gathers facts and impressions from his interlocutress, organizes and puts them into a broader social context than the heroine herself could do, and comments freely himself on the significance of the characters, incidents and social conditions.

The narrative perspective of *Kit* never really becomes objective, but Anderson controls it more effectively than he did in *Beyond Desire*. We move back and forth from the narrator's mind to Kit's and from an essayistic first person to a third-person point of view through which the main narrative strand operates. The result is confusion as to whose attitude and response we are getting, Kit's or the narrator's. Kit herself is indistinct, for, like other Andersonian protagonists, she is defined negatively; that is, she more often responds to than initiates action, she rejects most of the life she becomes involved in and ultimately runs away from it. We perceive her most commonly, therefore, in terms of her feelings of revulsion or compassion and her groping efforts to grasp the meaning of her experience.

Despite its technical defects, *Kit Brandon* has some remarkable episodes involving—once more—grotesque, defeated people. The story is based upon Anderson's experience at the trial of a gang of bootleggers and small-time still operators in the Virginia hills some fifty miles from Ripshin. Henry Morgenthau, then Secretary of the Treasury, telephoned Anderson from Washington and asked him to attend the trial and to report the full story of the people involved. Most of the still operators were poor farmers who had been arrested along with a large number of rumrunners. So many people were involved that it was apparent that bootlegging had become a way of life. "Big city gang methods had been introduced into the mountain community," Anderson recalled in "Man and His Imagination."[8] "Liquor was being made there in vast quantities. The whole county had been organized under one man and this man was a typical industrial overlord. He was ruling the county largely by terror and there were poor farmers in the county who had got into a situation where they were making liquor and turning it over to this man, themselves constantly facing the chances of a penitentiary sentence, for a wage of less than two dollars a day." Treasury agents investigated and put almost the whole county under arrest. Morgenthau felt that many of those arrested were poor and essentially innocent, and he wanted "the human story told."

The story of the rumrunners and the still-operators struck Anderson, when he observed the trial, as a microcosmic reconstruction of the history of capitalism in this country and as an epitome of the plight of the individual caught up in it. As he attended the trials, he became interested in a young woman who had been a rumrunner; and, during long automobile rides and dinner talks, he got her story, which became that of Kit Brandon. Kit's story is that of the dilemma of an innocent girl. She escapes from the animal crudity of mountain life only to be caught, like all of Anderson's heroes, in the corruption of an egoistic, mechanized civilization. She soon learns that the best things in life go to the acquisitive rather than to the virtuous and, trading on her beauty, gains those trappings of the good life by marrying the useless son of bootlegger baron Tom Halsey.

Growing bored with her loutish husband and with her insulated life, she becomes a rumrunner for her father-in-law, which satisfies an obsession for driving cars that serves her as a kind of grotesque substitute for the natural masculinity that has gone out of men in the modern age. The machine has a power and a kind of poetry she craves but cannot find in men. Toward them she maintains an attitude ranging from scorn for the ineffectual Gordon Halsey, to guarded respect for and fear of Tom Halsey, and tender solicitude—which resembles love—for three defeated young men of sensibility she meets at various times during the course of her wanderings.

Unlike her model, Dreiser's Carrie Meeber, Kit is a dimly outlined figure because we seldom see her from the outside. Once again, it is in the incidents involving minor characters—when Kit becomes the narrator—that Anderson best achieves his portrayals of cultural failure and of individual impotence and defeat. Flashes of the *Winesburg* pathos and grotesqueness appear, for instance, in an episode involving a sensitive young man who has left the hills to work in a mill, where he has contracted a fatal case of tuberculosis. Sensitive and quiet by nature, he has become bitter with the inexplicable evil in life and in nature that destroys innocence and draws simple hill folk to the factories, where they allow themselves to be exploited. Unsophisticated in his outlook, he curses the mill and the nebulous and indifferent "those" who own it. Brilliant also is the incident in which his hill friend, Bud, prances about on all fours like a horse—an act symbolizing the loss of natural sentience, beauty, and male strength by the industrial-age man. Counterpointing the symbol of the loss of masculine vigor is the ironic portrayal of Agnes, a woman of wild and crude female force whose intrinsic feminine gentleness and compassion cannot develop because, as a woman, she is compelled to assume the masculine role of leadership in the struggle to preserve humane values in the machine age.

Such episodes—and there are a number of outstanding ones—carry the theme of cultural failure with greater force and dramatic clarity than does the major narrative strand involving the fortunes of Kit herself. Torn from the soil, lacking "roots" in either nature or society, alienated from family and community, these characters present a picture of the dislocation and disjointedness that has come to be the accepted characteristics of the human condition in this century. The restless movement of Kit from the mountains to the factory, from store clerk to bored young matron, and from reckless rumrunner to pursued felon serves as a kind of *leitmotif* for the aimlessness and futility of a people cast adrift in the world. That Kit's narrative about herself seldom becomes more than a *leitmotif* is a measure of the failure of the book as a whole; but it is also an indication of the essential unity of its episodes. For, while Anderson fails through Kit to provide a single, sharply focused vision of a woman dissociated from the sources of her being in a dehumanized machine civilization, he does achieve an admirable series of revealing and thematically related moments in the lives of obscure, strangely twisted people. His last novel is a final confirmation of his mastery of the brief episode and of his inability to master the demands of the romance or of the novel.

CHAPTER *8*

The Summing Up

I The Memoirs

ANDERSON'S *Memoirs* were still unfinished when he died in 1941, and they are fragmentary in spite of Paul Rosenfeld's gallant editorial efforts to complete them. Confronted with a lack of material dealing with the last decade or so of Anderson's life, Rosenfeld filled in the open spaces by including selections he considered representative of the periods Anderson had not covered. In some instances—notably the section titled "The Death of Lawrence"—the selection, though admirable in itself, mars the unity of the book somewhat by shifting the emphasis from Anderson himself; but much of the book is done in the casual, chatty style—so deceptively easy to achieve— of the early Anderson.

Like Fitzgerald's uncompleted *Last Tycoon,* the *Memoirs* might have turned out to be comparable in quality to Anderson's finest work; for just as Fitzgerald regarded *Gatsby* as his masterpiece and consciously tried to recapture its lean, compressed style and spare, simple structure, so Anderson deliberately attempted to regain the cadenced rhythms and quiet conversational tone of *Winesburg,* of *Poor White,* and of his best tales and short selections. Like Fitzgerald, whose death two and a half months before Anderson's snapped off *The Last Tycoon* in the middle of the first draft, Anderson showed some promise of finding once more the technical and stylistic mastery of his salad days. But the greater tragedy was Fitzgerald's, for, while *The Last Tycoon* can never be anything more than a small portion of what might have been a great novel, the *Memoirs* is complete enough to have a narrative framework. Though Rosenfeld's selection of sketches filling in the vacant periods is by no means uniformly felicitous, the book has a pattern which gives it an overall unity despite the occasional lapses.

Its organizing principle is mythic, and the chief facts of Anderson's life merely serve as the skeletal outline of his psychological and moral pilgrimage as once again he takes us on that symbolic journey from youthful innocence to psychic illness and back to health, and then through the loss of a vulnerable, naïve innocence to the achievement of "wise" innocence in becoming a writer. His final role is that of the literary elder statesman who is admittedly past his prime but resigned enough to his loss of imaginative power to concede—with a good deal more modesty than accuracy—that "For all my egotism I know I am but a minor figure." The book is an affirmation that "Life, not death, is the great adventure," a motto he wished to have inscribed on his grave, but the theme is the usual Andersonian one that in twentieth-century America men have for some reason perversely destroyed the things that could bring joy to their lives. And, as he recalls the sources of his stories and techniques of writing and reminisces about his youth, his experiences in the towns and cities of the Middle West, and his literary acquaintances, he draws a discernible conflict between the powerful psychological and moral impulses toward imaginative integrity and the egoistic inclinations that were constantly at work undermining that wholeness he gained and strove to maintain as an artist.

The *Memoirs* should be read and judged as a work of fiction rather than as a piece of personal history, for it is a personal work of intense subjective impressions in which fact merges imperceptibly with fancy and becomes symbolic. Like *A Story Teller's Story*, it is strictly speaking a "confession" rather than an autobiography; it is basically an imaginative and not a factual recreation of his life. It relates the growth and integration of Anderson's imagination instead of an objective, factual reconstruction of his life. It is thus more akin to Joyce's *Portrait* than to a work like Franklin's *Autobiography,* and it is closer in purpose to St. Augustine's *Confessions* and to Sir Thomas Browne's *Religio Medici* than to Grant's *Memoirs*.

As a fictionalized autobiography it illustrates once more the fact that Anderson had only one sustained story to tell and that he told it over and over again in his full-length works: the story of his own life transformed into what he regarded as the composite fable of the "typical" American, the story we have identified as the myth of the American Adam. In retrospect, his own quest for psychic health, which made him a writer and served repeatedly as his narrative vehicle, had its origins, despite its apparent sophistication, in a primitivistic agrarianism that changed very little after 1912. Nothing better expresses the gist of Anderson's primitivism than the following passage, in which he tells of watching a group of Southern Negroes:

> I sat watching, drunk with all this as I have seldom been drunk. Long, long ago I had felt something of the soil in the Negro I had wanted in myself too.
>
> I mean a sense of earth and skies and trees and rivers, not as a thing thought about but as a thing in me. I wanted earth in me and skies and fields and rivers and people. I wanted these things to come out of me, as song, as singing prose, as poetry even.
>
> What else have I ever cared for as I have cared to have this happen, what woman, what possessions, what promise of life after death, all that? I have wanted this unity of things, this song, this earth, this sky, this human brotherhood.

What is this idea of the "unity of things" but the "concept of natural harmonies" extended into the social and psychological aspects of life and made into moral imperatives? Jefferson, Anderson maintained in the *Memoirs*, had come closer than anyone in America to building a civilization; but something else "came into being" that Jefferson would "have fought instinctively and hated." Anderson himself hated and fought the industrial age for the same reasons Jefferson undoubtedly would have: it meant the end of his dream of a nation of freehold farmers and tradesmen who were economically and politically independent and who lived harmoniously with a benevolent nature. Despite his frequent protests to the contrary, Anderson refused to accept the age of the machine; and, refusing to accept it as an accomplished fact, he was never able to judge it save in agrarian terms nor to combat it on social, political, and economic grounds. He relied always upon a morality whose chief tenet was that egoism—the cause of most of the problems of modern life, including industrial capitalism—would disappear if by simple assertion of will all men would become brothers. In his longer works of fiction, as in his own life, this meant that all he had to offer as alternatives to the mechanization and materialism he deplored were, by turns, the kind of aimless psychological collectivism we see in *Marching Men* and in *Beyond Desire* and a rediscovery of sex, such as appears in *Many Marriages* and *Dark Laughter*. Both of these alternatives are basically inner equivalents of the notion of natural harmonies, and, like the concept of natural harmonies, they are thoroughly romantic, socially impracticable, and intellectually indefensible.

Anderson's attitudes after 1912 remained basically unchanged. His heart lay in the rural simplicity of his youth, but it was the ideals rather than the facts, the feelings and the sentient newness of his Midwestern youth, that he wanted all his life to recapture. Armed with little more than a deep nostalgia for a way of life that could never be called back into being, he found in writing the sense of communion and sentient vitality he believed had been lost with the disappearance of the yeoman farmer and the tradesman. But his own regeneration could scarcely serve as a universal model; and, when he tried to prescribe sex and collectivism as workable popular alternatives to art, he invariably oversimplified both the nature and the problems of urban industrial society.

His thesis, to the end of his life, was that only a spiritual rebirth could save modern men from the machine; but he was never able to present his primitivistic modes of regeneration in convincing narrative terms. Unfortunately, he probably never read Thoreau, who might have taught him how to draw the ritual renewal of life in physical as well as in imaginative terms. The thematic parallels between *Walden* and—for example—*Many Marriages* are numerous: just as Thoreau was prepared to live "more lives" when he left Walden, so John Webster ostensibly becomes free to "live a hundred or a thousand lives"; just as

Thoreau maintained that "the mass of men lead lives of quiet desperation," Webster observes that, "as things are now, here in this town and in all other towns and cities I have ever been in, things are a good deal in a muddle. Everywhere lives are lived without purpose"; and just as Thoreau declares that he does not want to discover at the end of his life that he had not lived, Webster resolves not to live the kind of life in which "men and women . . . spend their lives going in and out of houses and factories . . . and find themselves at last facing death and the end of life without having lived at all." The similarity of themes accounts for a similarity in structure, for, like Thoreau, Webster achieves a "cleansing, a strange sort of renewal," and the ritualistic progression of both books grows quite naturally out of the similar primitivistic assumptions that modern man has lost touch with nature and must renew his connection with it if he is to be human.

But the difference between the soundness of Thoreau's and of Anderson's arguments is painfully apparent. In praising his archetype of the simple modern man with the virtues of nature unspoiled by an acquisitive society (the Canadian wood-chopper), Thoreau was fully conscious of the woodchopper's intellectual deficiencies. In his life at Walden he clearly recognized that the return to the simple life afforded an opportunity to utilize the mind as well as to bring all the senses to life and to sharpen the imagination. He based his primitivism on a genuine acquaintance with the past; and, in a style beautifully enriched with historical, philosophical, and classical allusions, Thoreau drew upon that past to cultivate the raw materials of nature as he found them.

Anderson, tragically, lacked Thoreau's intellectual range and depth, and his effort to bring the historical weight of the Christian tradition in support of his primitivistic theme of "blood consciousness" by means of the symbol of the Virgin is ridiculous. Similar attempts to bring sophisticated characters, style, and dialect together with primitivistic themes resulted in the failures of *Windy, Marching Men, Dark Laughter, Beyond Desire,* and *Kit Brandon.*

II *Achievement*

But Anderson's discouragingly long list of failures by no means diminishes the brilliance of his successes. If he failed as a sophisticated novelist, this failure was at least partly because he himself was not sophisticated, because he was a deeply involved purveyor of impressions and a man who suffered with his hurt and puzzled grotesques, and because he was not an intellectual or a detached observer and recorder of manners. The range of his materials was admittedly narrow; but, if he was limited to Adamic heroes and grotesques, he mined his literary quarry intensively. No other writer has portrayed so movingly the emerging consciousness of the culturally under-privileged Midwesterner and has done it, for the most part, with neither condescension nor satiric caricature.

Anderson's impact upon younger writers was such that it has left a permanent mark upon most of the major American fiction of this century. In a now-famous interview in 1956, William Faulkner declared that Anderson was "the father of my gener-ation of American writers and the tradition of American writing which our successors will carry on." Faulkner repeated that conviction two years later when he told a gathering of students at the University of Virginia that Anderson "has never been given his rightful place in American literature. In my opinion he's the father of all my generation—Hemingway, Erskine Cald-well, Thomas Wolfe, Dos Passos." Twain, of course, was the grandfather of them all; but "Sherwood Anderson . . . has still to receive his rightful place in American letters."[1]

Faulkner's high regard for Anderson was perhaps prompted in part by affection for the loyal, generous friend who had helped launch his career as a writer and who had portrayed Faulkner touchingly in one of his finest stories, "A Meeting South." But the facts support Faulkner's comment about Ander-son's influence on younger writers, particularly in the early years. The ancestors of Faulkner's own Yoknapatawpha citizens are the grotesques of Anderson's *Winesburg, Ohio*. Ernest Hemingway, who also acknowledged Mark Twain's *Huck Finn* as the progenitor of modern American fiction, served his apprenticeship under the aegis of Sherwood Anderson; and, though Hemingway took some of his lessons in literary theory from Gertrude Stein, the much admired "Hemingway style" drew its earliest impulses from Anderson's deceptively simple, matter-of-fact, and direct Midwestern sentences. And while Thomas Wolfe, with characteristic rudeness, ended his friendship with Anderson shortly after they met, Wolfe readily acknowledged his debt to Anderson; and one can hardly fail to see strong similarities between Anderson's young George Willard of *Winesburg, Ohio* and his Windy McPherson of *Windy McPherson's Son* and Wolfe's Eugene and Oliver Gant in *Look Homeward, Angel.*

Anderson's great influence upon many of the major figures in twentieth-century American writing is clear and well known. Others indebted to him include Hart Crane, John Steinbeck, and William Saroyan. For all these writers, Anderson opened new perspectives in subject matter as well as narrative technique and style. He also brought into twentieth-century fiction the symbolic techniques for introspective and intuitive exploration of the inner life that Whitman had achieved for poetry in the nineteenth century and that Stephen Crane had begun to use before his death in 1900. Like Twain and Whitman, Anderson found obscure "little" people a vast and eminently worthy source of literary material through which to explore the tensions in American culture. Perhaps his most significant achievement as a writer was his ability to present with penetrating insight the intense moments of happiness, defeat, triumph, or revelation—the discovery of spirit—as they impinge upon the uncomplicated minds of simple, innocent, inhibited, and hitherto inarticulate people who have neither "fallen" into the egoistic realm of success nor gained the mature, "wise" innocence of the Adamic hero. Where those moments combined with a lyrical tone of reminiscence or confession to reveal the strange, sad instants of awareness that come to young men or women as they move from the moral certainty of youth to the difficult adult world of ambiguities and paradoxes, Anderson gave us portrayals of the inner life second to none in our literature. Such moments are evoked in *Winesburg, Ohio,* in "The Egg," in "The Man Who Became a Woman," in "Death in the Woods," and in "I Want to Know Why," masterpieces that are not unworthy of comparison with the best achievements of Twain, Chekhov, Turgenev, Faulkner, and Hemingway.

No one would be likely to deny, therefore, the truth of Faulkner's comment about Anderson's influence upon the American fiction of this century. His statement about Anderson's place in American letters, however, is at least open to question; for, though Anderson's reputation is not by any means as high as it was at the peak of his success during the mid-1920's, it is not so low as it was at the time of his death in 1941. Then Lionel Trilling—expressing, surely, the feeling of many responsible critics who had seen Anderson's steady decline—wrote of the "residue of admiration" he still felt for Anderson even though Anderson had long since ceased to be an "immediate force" in his life. The fact is that Anderson's position as an important figure in American literature is a secure one, for *Winesburg, Ohio* and several of his tales are well established as classic works which, unlike many other classics, are widely read; and while he admittedly left a relatively small body of first-rate work, the quality of that work has assured him a most significant and enduring place in the literature of the twentieth century.

Notes and References

Chapter One

1. Besides *Windy McPherson's Son* and *Marching Men* he had completed *Mary Cochran* and *Talbot Whittingham*.
2. Irving Howe, *Sherwood Anderson* (New York, 1951), p. 7.
3. *Sherwood Anderson's Memoirs* (New York, 1942), p. 13.
4. *A Story Teller's Story* (New York, 1924), p. 4. (See also Grove Press paperback reprint.)
5. *Ibid.*, p. 155.
6. *Ibid.*
7. James Schevill, *Sherwood Anderson: His Life and Work* (University of Denver Press, 1951), p. 29.
8. *Ibid.*, p. 28.
9. Howe, *op. cit.*, p. 31.
10. *Memoirs*, p. 34.
11. *Ibid.*
12. *Ibid.*, pp. 188-199.
13. Schevill, *op. cit.*, p. 49. Cited from Wm. Sutton.
14. Ben Hecht, "Go, Scholar Gypsy," *Story*, XIX, 19 (Sept.-Oct., 1941), 90-92.
15. *Memoirs*, p. 243.
16. *Story*, XIX, 19 (Sept.-Oct., 1941), 35. For full treatment of the Freudian influence upon Anderson's works see Frederick Hoffman's *Freudianism and the Literary Mind*, pp. 229-57. See also Trigant Burrow's letters to William L. Philips in *A Search for Man's Sanity* (New York, 1958), pp. 558-62 for Burrow's statement of his own probable influence upon Anderson's psychological ideas in their discussions of Freud in 1916.
17. *Ibid.*, p. 38.
18. See Burrow's letter to Hoffman in *Freudianism and the Literary Mind.* p. 236.
19. Howard M. Jones and Walter B. Rideout, eds., *The Letters of Sherwood Anderson* (Boston, 1953), p. 49.
20. *Ibid.*, p. 51.
21. *Ibid.*, p. 79.
22. *The Autobiography of Alice B. Toklas* (New York, 1933), p. 197.
23. Schevill, *op. cit.*, p. 147.

24. See Charles A. Fenton, *The Apprenticeship of Ernest Hemingway: The Early Years.* (New York, 1958), p. 149.

25. *Letters,* p. 179.

26. *Ibid.,* p. 145.

27. *Ibid.,* p. 160.

28. *Ibid.,* p. 200.

29. *Ibid.,* p. 219.

30. The most notable instance was in 1932 when he joined Edmund Wilson and a number of other writers in signing "Culture and the Crisis," a document supporting William Z. Foster, Communist Party candidate for President.

31. *Letters,* p. 243.

32. *Ibid.,* p. 400.

33. *Ibid.,* p. 340.

34. *Ibid.,* p. 465.

Chapter Two

1. *Letters,* p. 104.

2. *Letters,* p. 33.

3. R. W. B. Adams, *The American Adam: Innocence, Tragedy, and Tradition in the Nineteenth Century* (Chicago, 1955), pp. 127-28.

4. See Frederic I. Carpenter, " 'The American Myth': Paradise (To Be) Regained," *PMLA,* LXXIV, 5 (Dec., 1959), 599-606.

5. Lewis, 154.

6. Richard Hofstadter, *The Age of Reform* (New York, 1955), p. 62.

7. See Henry Nash Smith's *Virgin Land: The American West as Symbol and Myth* (Cambridge, 1950), Ch. XVI, "The Garden and the Desert."

8. The Populist platform, as written by Ignatius Donnelly and presented to the convention in Omaha on July 4, 1892, was an indictment of both the Democratic and the Republican parties:

> We meet in the midst of a nation brought to the verge of moral, political, and material ruin. Corruption dominates the ballotbox, the legislatures, the Congress, and touches even the ermine of the bench. The people are demoralized; . . . The newspapers are largely subsidized or muzzled; public opinion silenced; business prostrated; our homes covered with mortgages; labor impoverished; and the land concentrating in the hands of the capitalists. The urban workmen are denied the right of organization for self-protection; imported pauperized labor beats down their wages; a hireling standing army, unrecognized by our laws, is established to shoot them down, and they are rapidly degenerating into European conditions. The fruits of the toil of millions are bodily stolen to build up colossal fortunes for a few, unprecedented in the history of mankind; and the possessors

of those in turn, despise the republic and endanger liberty. From the same prolific womb of governmental injustice we breed the two great classes — tramps and millionaires.

9. Hofstadter, *op. cit.*, p. 92 and note.
10. *Memoirs*, p. 284.
11. *The Anatomy of Criticism* (Princeton University Press, 1957), pp. 303-14.

Chapter Three

1. *Letters*, p. 39.
2. *A Story Teller's Story*, p. 360.
3. *Memoirs*, p. 243.
4. For an excellent elaboration of this point, see Edwin Fussell's analysis of *Winesburg* in "*Winesburg, Ohio*: Art and Isolation," *Modern Fiction Studies*, VI, 2 (Summer, 1960), 106-14.

Chapter Four

1. *Letters*, p. 37.
2. *Ibid.*, p. 54.
3. *Ibid.*, p. 43.
4. *Ibid.*, p. 33.
5. *Ibid.*, p. 40.

Chapter Five

1. Paul Rosenfeld, *Port of New York* (New York, 1924), p. 183.
2. For a full discussion of Anderson's handling of point of view in these tales, see Irving Howe's chapter on the short stories in *Sherwood Anderson*.
3. As Lionel Trilling implies it is, in *The Liberal Imagination*, p. 26.

Chapter Six

1. *Letters*, p. 43.
2. For a full discussion of Adams' primitivism see James Baird, *Ishmael: A Study of the Symbolic Mode in Primitivism* (New York, 1960), pp. 141-48.
3. *Letters*, p. 144.
4. *Freudianism and the Literary Mind.* See Chapter VI, "Lawrence's Quarrel with Freud." See also Trilling's *The Liberal Imagination* and Howe on this issue of Lawrence's acquaintance with ideas and Anderson's lack of intellectual background.
5. *Ibid.*, pp. 89-90.
6. *Ibid.*, p. 236. See Burrow's letter to Hoffman of October 2, 1942.
7. See Burrow's letter to William L. Philips, *A Search for Man's*

Sanity (New York, 1958), p. 559. In this letter Burrow corrects his earlier statement to Hoffman that Anderson had not been influenced by the ideas of Freud, saying that it was likely that Burrow's own comments on Freud probably had considerable influence on Anderson.

8. *Ibid.*

9. Northrop Frye, *op. cit.*, p. 308.

10. Carpenter, *op. cit.*, p. 606.

Chapter Seven

1. Schevill, *op. cit.*, p. 209.

2. *Letters*, p. 198.

3. *Ibid.*, pp. 198-99.

4. *Ibid.*, p. 213.

5. *Ibid.*, p. 207.

6. *Ibid.*, p. 335.

7. *Ibid.*, p. 331.

8. In *The Intent of the Artist*, ed. Augusto Centeno (Princeton, 1941), p. 55.

Chapter Eight

1. Quoted from *Writers at Work: The Paris Review Interviews*, ed. Malcolm Cowley (New York, 1959), p. 135.

Selected Bibliography

The best bibliographical listing to date is *Sherwood Anderson: A Bibliography* by Eugene Sheehy and Kenneth Lohf (Los Gatos, California: Talisman Press, 1960). An earlier compilation of Anderson's own works was made by Raymond D. Gozzi and published in December, 1948, in the Anderson Memorial Number, *The Newberry Library Bulletin*.

PRIMARY SOURCES

(Listed Chronologically)

Windy McPherson's Son. New York: John Lane Company, 1916.

Marching Men. New York: John Lane Company, 1917.

Mid-American Chants. New York: John Lane Company, 1918.

Winesburg, Ohio. New York: B. W. Heubsch, Inc., 1919. Reprints: Viking Compass; Signet; Modern Library.

Poor White. New York: B. W. Heubsch, Inc., 1920. Reprint: Viking *Portable Anderson*.

Triumph of the Egg. New York: B. W. Heubsch, Inc., 1921.

Many Marriages. New York: B. W. Heubsch, Inc., 1923.

Horses and Men. New York: B. W. Heubsch, Inc., 1923.

A Story Teller's Story. New York: B. W. Heubsch, Inc., 1924.

Dark Laughter. New York: Boni and Liveright, 1925.

The Modern Writer. New York: Gelber, Lilienthal, 1925.

Sherwood Anderson's Notebook. New York: Boni and Liveright, 1926.

Tar: A Midwest Childhood. New York: Boni and Liveright, 1926.

A New Testament. New York: Boni and Liveright, 1927.

Hello Towns. New York: Liveright Publishing Corporation, 1929.

Perhaps Women. New York: Liveright Publishing Corporation, 1931.

Beyond Desire. New York: Liveright Publishing Corporation, 1932.

Death in the Woods. New York: Liveright Publishing Corporation, 1933.

No Swank. Philadelphia: The Centaur Press, 1934.

Puzzled America. New York: Charles Scribner's Sons, 1935.

Kit Brandon. New York: Charles Scribner's Sons, 1936.

Plays: Winesburg and Others. New York: Charles Scribner's Sons, 1937.

Home Town. Alliance Book Corporation, 1940.

Sherwood Anderson's Memoirs. New York: Harcourt, Brace and Company, 1942.

Selected Bibliography

The Sherwood Anderson Reader. New York: Houghton, Mifflin Company, 1948.
The Portable Sherwood Anderson. New York: Viking Press, 1949.
Letters of Sherwood Anderson. New York: Little, Brown and Company. 1953.

SECONDARY SOURCES

An abundance of excellent criticism and scholarship on Anderson, as well as a number of fine personal reminiscences, exists. The following selections represent, generally, the best and the most accessible. Especially recommended among the articles are those by Waldo Frank, Paul Rosenfeld, Horace Gregory, Howard Mumford Jones, and Malcolm Cowley. Lionel Trilling's famous piece is still required reading for those who wish to keep Anderson in a balanced perspective. Of the full-length works, Irving Howe's study assesses Anderson against the highest literary standards and is the best comprehensive treatment to date, though it is not by any means entirely sympathetic, and its author's brilliance at times obscures rather than illuminates his subject. James Schevill's book is less critical than Howe's but more sympathetic and more valuable as biography. Cleveland Chase's *Sherwood Anderson* (1928) is now generally out of date, though much of what Chase says has become standard interpretation. Walter B. Rideout is at work on a much-needed definitive biography of Anderson.

Books about Sherwood Anderson:

HOWE, IRVING. *Sherwood Anderson.* New York: Wm. Sloane Associates, 1951. Best full-length critical treatment of Anderson to date, though not an entirely sympathetic work.
SCHEVILL, JAMES. *Sherwood Anderson: His Life and Work.* Denver: The Denver University Press, 1951. A thorough survey of Anderson's life and works but frequently uncritical.

Articles and chapters of books discussing Anderson:

ANDERSON, MARGARET. *My Thirty Years War.* New York: Covici, Friede, Inc., 1930. Recollections by the editor of the *Little Review.*
BEACH, JOSEPH WARREN. *The Outlook for American Prose.* Chicago: University of Chicago Press, 1926. Still the best study of Andersons use of the naïve style.
BUDD, LOUIS J. "The Grotesques of Anderson and Wolfe," *Modern Fiction Studies,* V (Winter, 1959-60), 304-10. Shows Anderson's influence on Wolfe.
CARGILL, OSCAR. "The Primitivists." *Intellectual America: Ideas on the March.* New York: Macmillan, 1941. Discusses the nature of Anderson's cultural primitivism.

COWLEY, MALCOLM. "Anderson's Lost Days of Innocence," *New Republic*, CXLII (Feb. 15, 1960), 16-18.

————. Introduction. *Winesburg, Ohio*. New York: Viking Press, 1960. First-rate discussions by a literary historian and critic who both understands and sympathizes with Anderson.

DUFFEY, BERNARD. "The Struggle for Affirmation—Anderson, Sandburg, Lindsay." *The Chicago Renaissance in American Letters*. Lansing: Michigan State University Press, 1954. Puts Anderson within the framework of the whole Chicago movement, which Anderson called the "robin's-egg renaissance."

FAULKNER, WILLIAM. "Sherwood Anderson: An Appreciation," *Atlantic*, CXCI (June, 1953), 27-29. Faulkner's comments are sympathetic but by no means uncritical.

FRANK, WALDO. "*Winesburg, Ohio* after Twenty Years," *Story*, XXIX (Sept.-Oct., 1941), 29-33. Puts Anderson's work in its cultural setting. One of the best pieces on Anderson by a friend of many years.

FRIEND, JULIUS. "The Philosophy of Sherwood Anderson," *Story*, XXIX (Sept.-Oct., 1941), 37-41. Defines Anderson's philosophy of brotherhood.

FUSSELL, EDWIN. "*Winesburg, Ohio:* Art and Isolation," *Modern Fiction Studies*, VI (Summer, 1960), 106-14. An outstanding analysis of the nature of loneliness in the grotesques.

GALANTIERE, LEWIS. "French Reminiscence," *Story*, XXIX (Sept.-Oct., 1941), 64-67. Recalls Anderson's first visit to Paris with Tennessee Anderson and Paul Rosenfeld.

GEISMAR, MAXWELL. "Sherwood Anderson: Last of the Townsmen." *The Last of the Provincials: The American Novel, 1915-1925*. Boston: Houghton, Mifflin Company, 1947. Geismar makes some penetrating observations, but he is often intemperate in his judgments.

GOLD, HERBERT. "*Winesburg, Ohio:* The Purity and Cunning of Sherwood Anderson," *Hudson Review*, X (Winter, 1957-58), 548-57. Reprinted: Shapiro, Charles, ed. *Twelve Original Essays on Great American Novels*. Detroit: Wayne State University Press, 1958. Suggestive but somewhat impressionistic.

GREGORY, HORACE. Introduction to *The Portable Sherwood Anderson*. New York: Viking Press, 1949. Recommended as one of the best critical pieces on Anderson.

HANSEN, HARRY. "Anderson in Chicago," *Story*, XXIX (Sept.-Oct., 1941), 34-36. Tells of Anderson's bohemian days during the period when he wrote *Winesburg, Ohio*.

————. "Sherwood Anderson: Corn-fed Mystic, Historian of the Middle Age of Man." *Midwest Portraits*. New York: Harcourt, 1923. Discusses Anderson's middle-aged heroes and breaks with convention.

Selected Bibliography

HARTWICK, HARRY. "Broken Face Gargoyles." *The Foreground of American Fiction*. New York: The American Book Company, 1934. A standard work on the grotesques in Anderson's fiction.

HATCHER, HARLAN. "Freudian Psychology and the Sex Age." *Creating the Modern American Novel*. New York: Farrar and Rinehart, 1935. Anderson himself thought highly of Hatcher's discussion of his work.

HECHT, BEN. "Go, Scholar-Gypsy," *Story*, XXIX (Sept.-Oct., 1941), 92-93. More reminiscences of the Chicago days.

HOFFMAN, FREDERICK. *Freudianism and the Literary Mind*. Baton Rouge: Louisiana State University Press, 1957. Reprinted: Evergreen Books. Hoffman's treatment of Anderson's psychological themes is first-rate.

JONES, HOWARD MUMFORD, with WALTER B. RIDEOUT. Introduction, *Letters of Sherwood Anderson*. Boston: Little, Brown and Company, 1953. The letters themselves are indispensable to the student of Anderson; fascinating to the general reader.

KAZIN, ALFRED. "The New Realism — Sherwood Anderson and Sinclair Lewis." *On Native Grounds*. New York: Reynal and Hitchcock, 1942. Places Anderson among those who spoke for the "new liberation."

LEWIS, WYNDHAM. "Paleface: (12) Sherwood Anderson," *The Enemy*, II (Sept., 1928), 26-27. An early attack on Anderson's primitivism and anti-intellectualism.

LOVETT, ROBERT MORSS. "Sherwood Anderson," *New Republic*, LXXXIX (Nov. 25, 1936), 103-5. Reprinted: Cowley, Malcolm, ed. *After the Genteel Tradition*. New York: Norton, 1937. An appreciation.

—————. "Sherwood Anderson, American," *Virginia Quarterly Review*, XVII (Summer, 1941), 379-88. Reprinted: Zabel, Morton Dauwen, ed. *Literary Opinion in America*. Rev. ed. New York: Harper, 1951. Shows Anderson as an indigenous writer.

PARRINGTON, VERNON L. "Sherwood Anderson: A Psychological Naturalist." *Main Currents of American Thought*. New York: Harcourt, Brace, 1930. Shows Anderson bringing naturalism into the realm of the mind in the Age of Freud.

PEARSON, NORMAN HOLMES. "Anderson and the New Puritanism," *Newberry Library Bulletin*, II (Dec., 1948), 52-63. Discusses the latent Puritanism in Anderson's moral fervor.

PHILIPS, WILLIAM L. "How Sherwood Anderson wrote *Winesburg, Ohio*," *American Literature*, XXIII (March, 1951), 7-30. A valuable piece of scholarship showing Anderson's debt to Masters and proving he carefully organized the tales to fit an over-all design.

RINGE, DONALD A. "Point of View and Theme in 'I Want to Know

Why,'" *Critique*, (Spring-Fall, 1959), pp. 24-29. Shows importance of controlled perspective to the meaning of the tale.

ROSENFELD, PAUL. "Sherwood Anderson." *Port of New York*. New York: Harcourt, Brace and Company, 1924.

————. "The Man of Good Will," *Story*, XXIX (Sept.-Oct., 1941), 5-10.

————. Introduction. *The Sherwood Anderson Reader*. Boston: Houghton Mifflin Company, 1947. A sympathetic friend, Rosenfeld was also an astute critic, as these essays on Anderson reveal.

SERGEL, ROGER. "The Man and the Memory," *The Newberry Library Bulletin*, II (Dec., 1948), 44-51. Reminiscences by a Chicago friend.

SUTTON, WILLIAM A. *Sherwood Anderson's Formative Years*, (1876-1913). Ph.D. dissertation, Ohio State University, 1943.

TRILLING, LIONEL. "Sherwood Anderson." *The Liberal Imagination*. New York: Viking Press, 1950. Reprinted: Anchor Books, 1958. Presents a strong case for the view that Anderson is of minor importance as a writer.

WALCUTT, CHARLES C. "Sherwood Anderson: Impressionism and the Buried Life," *The Sewanee Review*, LX (Jan.-Mar., 1952), 28-47. Reprinted: *American Literary Naturalism: A Divided Stream*. Minneapolis: University of Minnesota Press, 1956. The best exposition of Anderson's impressionistic techniques and style.

WEST, RAY B. *The Short Story in America*. Chicago: Henry Regnery, 1952. Brief discussion of the moral assumptions in Anderson's themes.

WINTHUR, S. K. "The Aura of Loneliness in Sherwood Anderson," *Modern Fiction Studies*, V (Summer, 1959), 145-52. Examines loneliness as a major theme. Compare with the article by Edwin Fussell listed above.

Index

Index

Index